Make
It
Happen

Manifest the life
of your dreams

Jordanna Levin

murdoch books
Sydney | London

PRAISE FOR MAKE IT HAPPEN

'This book is a "must read" for anyone wanting to create change in their life. Whether you are finding yourself stuck in any area of life, or all of them, Jordanna's writing speaks to your heart and your mind with so many "uh-huh" moments. With a real-life approach to creating the life you want to live, this book is funny, relatable and life changing. Within one week of following this principle and doing the "work", three of my six intentions had started to come to life. Mind blown... the manifestation equation works. I cannot recommend this highly enough.'

—Charlie de Haas, founder and creative director
of the Clean Treats Factory

'*Make It Happen* isn't just a book about manifestation. This book encompasses all things soul, love and navigating life from a place of alignment, purpose and intention. Jordanna Levin is a breath of fresh air, teaming humour with profound wisdom. Her words had me laughing, crying and yelling yes while fist-pumping in the air. If you are serious about up-levelling your life, ready to call in your soulmate or dream career—or just curious about why life happens the way it does—this is the book for you.'

—Hollie Azzopardi, life coach and author of
The People Pleaser's Guide to Putting Yourself First

'We can all manifest the life of our dreams but it takes conscious awareness to make it happen, and the beautiful thing about Jordanna is that she will hold your hand and show you how. Just like a best friend, she guides you toward creating your dream life.'

—Melissa Ambrosini, bestselling author of
Mastering Your Mean Girl

'Witty, practical and laugh-out-loud funny, this is a book you'll want to keep close by as you manifest what means the most to you. Jordanna will help you focus your energy, thoughts and actions in a way that will support you to create whatever it is you're wanting to create, and along the way, you'll realise that the power to do so was already—and always will be—inside you.'

—Cassie Mendoza-Jones, bestselling author of *You Are Enough*

'Reading this book was like being in one of Jordanna's workshops; I connected with the part of me that feels safe, capable, creative, inspired and able to spark into action. I went through a divorce this year and I can honestly say that the information contained within these pages was directly responsible for me being able to buy the house of my dreams, hold space for my kids in the transition and step up work to meet my new income needs. If you have any dreams or goals, buy this book and watch them unfold into being.'

—Katie Manitsas, yoga instructor, Wise Earth School of Ayurveda master teacher, doula and author

'Finally, a book that explains manifestation in a real-world way! Exploring the power of positive thought and the importance of practical action, this guide will win over spiritualists and skeptics alike. The perfect mix of grounded advice, easy-to-follow steps and a reminder to believe in magic. I'll be gifting this book to my friends, whether they have faith or not.'

—Amy Molloy, author of *The World Is a Nice Place*

This edition published in 2021 by Murdoch Books, an imprint of Allen & Unwin
First published in 2019 by Murdoch Books

Murdoch Books UK
Ormond House, 26–27 Boswell Street, London WC1N 3JZ
Phone: +44 (0) 20 8785 5995
murdochbooks.co.uk
info@murdochbooks.co.uk

A catalogue record for this book is available from the British Library

ISBN 978 1 92235 146 3 UK

Cover and text design by Arielle Gamble
Printed and bound by CPI Group (UK) Ltd, Croydon, CR04YY

10 9 8 7 6 5

MIX
Paper from
responsible sources
FSC
www.fsc.org
FSC® C171272

NOTE: The names of all the individuals in this
book have been changed to save them (and me)
from awkward run-ins at the supermarket.

This book is dedicated to my beautiful mama:
I let you think you were helping me write
a different dedication so that I could surprise
you with this one. #trickedya

CHAPTER 1

What Is the Manifestation Equation?

The Manifestation Equation is something I came up with after years of experimenting with my own manifestation practice and tweaking my approach to it. Only when I applied each of the equation's four parts to my practice did I receive the results I'd been searching for. I'll walk you through it soon enough, and teach you how to apply each element of the equation to any area or situation in your life. But for now, all you need to know is that the equation goes like this:

Thoughts + Feelings + Actions + Faith = Successful manifestation

Seems pretty straightforward, right? It is. This equation is based on four universal laws (we'll get to those soon), and I'll spend the first half of this book breaking this equation down for you bit by bit so it becomes even clearer. But first, let's take a little trip down the misguided manifestation path you've most likely wandered down.

WE'VE ONLY BEEN SOLD PART OF THE STORY

The danger when a concept like manifestation catches fire and becomes the spiritual 'it' thing (as this did around the mid-1990s) is that it can get watered down and oversimplified in the process of being packaged up for a mass market with a limited attention span. This was definitely true of poor manifestation, and it emerged from its moment in the spotlight a shadow of its former self. So even if you *think* you're familiar with the concepts and practices of manifesting, I'm going to ask you to put those ideas to one side until you've finished this book. You might find the recipe you've been sold is not the whole story. Not by a long shot.

The Law of Attraction

Don't get me wrong; I'm a big fan of the Law of Attraction. In fact, it's one of the four universal laws that the Manifestation Equation is based on. At its most basic level, the Law of Attraction states that **positive thoughts create a positive outcome, and negative thoughts create a negative outcome.**

I was first introduced to this law through the work of Esther Hicks. If you're not familiar with her work, perhaps you've heard of the spiritual entity known as Abraham through whom she receives her teachings? (Annnd I probably lost a whole bunch of you right there, with that one sentence.) If you aren't familiar, I encourage you to explore her work and make your own mind up.

This law became more mainstream in the mid-90s thanks to the hype that erupted around a certain 'secretive' book and the movie that followed. These piqued everyone's interest thanks to the wildly successful manifestation stories they featured—stories cloaked in veils of ease, zero effort and lucratively endorsed by Hollywood's elite (the most credible endorsement there is, no?).

The idea that our thoughts, positive or negative, produce positive or negative outcomes is, in essence, not untrue. HOWEVER, thoughts alone are not enough (more on this in Chapter 3). Think about it: if all of our thoughts manifested into reality, we'd be living in one crazy, messed up world! The real secret here, folks, is that the Law of Attraction on its own isn't a foolproof tool for manifestation.

Vision boards

Ooh, I love me a vision board. In fact, I have one up on my bedroom wall right now. But do they work as a sole *(or soul)* tool for manifestation? I'm going to have to say nope! Visualising your dream future is definitely a key part of manifestation, but staring at pictures and words of your dreams takes a critical piece out of the manifestation puzzle: YOU. What actions are you taking to bring those magazine clippings to life? Most vision boards remain unchanged for years, and the same reason applies here as with the Law of Attraction; simply visualising your manifestations isn't enough to make them a reality. (Soz, Oprah. Still love ya!)

Trusting in divine guidance and universal support

Yes, the universe most definitely has our back, and working alongside the universe is a key component of the Manifestation Equation (more on this when we dive into Chapter 6). But the trap that many people fall into is putting all their eggs in the universe's basket and relinquishing responsibility for their lives. I like to think of divine guidance and universal support as an even trade; you do your bit, and the universe will meet you halfway.

The Manifestation Equation is a four-part sum. Each part plays an integral role, but the critical piece, and one I left out for such a long time when I first started trying to manifest positive outcomes, is action—the role that I played in creating my own dream life. If you're not willing to take ownership for your future, and if you're not ready to admit that you create everything that is happening in your life, then manifestation *will* evade you.

For such a long time I thought the thoughts, felt the feels and trusted that the universe knew what was best for me, but still ... nothing! I felt like a failure until I realised that everything in my life wasn't happening *to* me, I was making it happen. It was time to start making things happen my way, on my terms, playing by my rules.

ENTER THE MANIFESTATION EQUATION

Where science abides by a bunch of natural laws (physics, biology, astronomy and chemistry), there is also a set of spiritual laws known as the 12 Universal Laws, and these govern everything in the universe. The Manifestation Equation is based on four of these laws.

1. **The Law of Attraction**

   We touched on this one earlier. Essentially it teaches that **like attracts like** and, more specifically, that thoughts play a vital role in the manifestation process. On its own, the Law of Attraction isn't enough to manifest successfully, but it's definitely a worthy participant in the Manifestation Equation and it's the basis for the first part of the equation: thoughts.

2. **The Law of Vibration**

   This is my personal favourite of the universal laws. It states that **everything in the universe vibrates on its own frequency, and that things with a similar frequency are drawn together.** You, me, inanimate objects, bacteria, diseases … EVERYTHING in the universe vibrates on its own frequency. And the easiest way to shift our own vibrations is through our feelings. (We'll explore this further in Chapter 4.)

3. **The Law of Action**

   Perhaps the most practical of all of the universal laws, this law states **you must do the things and perform the actions necessary to achieve what you are setting out to do.** Seems legit! And, as you'll soon learn as we progress through this book, this one is a non-negotiable law in manifestation.

4. **The Law of Rhythm**

   All energy in the universe is like a pendulum. It ebbs and flows, waxes and wanes, rises and falls, grows and decays. This is the Law of Rhythm, and it can be applied to anything you're trying to manifest. My introduction to manifestation was actually through the rhythm of the lunar cycle; this opened me up to the beauty and wisdom of all universal cycles by showing me what they can teach us about successful manifestation. We'll deep-dive into this when we explore faith in Chapter 6.

The Manifestation Equation was inspired by these four universal laws, but the four parts of my equation—thoughts, feelings, actions and faith—came to be through my own (often failed) experiments with manifestation.

LET'S TAKE A TRIP DOWN MY MANIFESTATION MEMORY LANE

When I was twenty-two, I started walking the 'think positive thoughts' path after reading Esther Hicks, and this did shift my mindset monumentally. I found myself seeing people and problems in a new light and creating wonderful opportunities by not always expecting the worst from every situation. It wasn't like I'd been walking around like Debbie Downer before this, but somewhere along the way I must have thought that expecting the worst would help cushion the blow of disappointment. By shifting my perspective to expect the best (or at least better), I found situations resulted in better outcomes.

But thinking the good thoughts all the time gave me bouts of serious anxiety. If I was creating wonderful things with positive thoughts, what would happen if I had a negative thought? The stress of thinking only beneficial thoughts had me spending WAY too much time in my head.

I needed to be in my body.

It was around this time that yoga entered my life. I'd been doing yoga for three years prior, but it was just another form of exercise; there was zero mind–body connection. But, if you stick with yoga long enough, you'll often find that one teacher who gives you the aha moment the ancient yogis of India prayed we'd all discover one day. Mine came in the form of a handsome (which totally helped), conscious and deeply spiritual teacher called Dan. My yoga awakening didn't come during a peak pose or a blissful savasana, or in the middle of one of Dan's frequently muttered philosophical yogic musings, it came in the middle of a dimly lit morning class full of yogis preparing themselves for a day at their desk jobs in the city (myself included).

I was all up in my head that morning. I was dreading going into work, belly deep in a hopeless on again/off again relationship, and overly concerned about how my butt looked in my Lululemon tights. While entering the simplest of poses, what should have been an easy transition quickly declined into excruciating pain as my right shoulder completely dislocated from its socket, leaving my arm hanging limply at my side.

As I wailed and collapsed from the shock and the pain (oh, the pain!), Dan, ever the zen yogi, calmly made his way over to my mat.

He instructed the class to continue with their practice (excuse me, what?!), wrapped me firmly in a blanket to keep my shoulder in place and asked me with gentle authority to focus on nothing but my breath. I'm not proud of the expletives that came out of my mouth that day, but as I (and 30 other yogis, plus Dan) waited for the paramedics to arrive with their green whistle and stretcher, I became so engrossed in the rhythm of my breath and its ability to relax the spasms in my muscles (turns out when your shoulder dislocates, your intelligent bod spasms involuntarily to try and relocate it) that the pain was far less excruciating. My heart rate returned to normal, and I discovered the power of vibrational energy and the breath on both the physical body and the mind.

The physicality of yoga combined with pranayama (conscious breathing) helped me discover the power of feelings and vibrations on manifestations. I found that when I connected my breath and movement to the thought processes I'd had success with in my earlier manifesting days, things manifested faster and with more conviction. Not into yoga? Don't worry. Yoga was just my entry point to understanding the importance of embodying the practice of manifestation, and of marrying physical action with thought. I'm going to teach you how to manifest without moving a muscle, if you so choose.

But that shoulder dislocation was so much more than my introduction to the breath. It was a massive wake-up call telling me that if I continued to ignore the toxicity in my working life and my relationships, and if I continued to neglect my own self-care, I was going to continue to create experiences such as this in order to learn these lessons again and again. And boy, did that lesson take me a while to learn—four more shoulder dislocations to be exact.

The next dislocation occurred when I allowed myself to go back to a toxic romantic relationship 'one last time'. Another happened while working sixty-hour weeks for a female narcissist and ignoring all the signs that were screaming at me to get the hell out of there. The next dislocation occurred after blatant disregard for my own self-worth resulted in me falling further and further into financial debt. The final one, the dislocation to end all dislocations, came while pushing myself so goddamn hard at the gym because I thought the size of my thighs was so much more important than my own mental health. When a dumbbell I was shoulder pressing came crashing down on my face, I suffered another dislocation and a black eye. I realised it was time for me to sort this shit out!

At this point, the sceptic would say, 'Oi! Halfwit! Your shoulder keeps dislocating because you ripped all of the ligaments and tendons that hold it together.' And they would be right, but these dislocations also *always* coincided with times in my life when I needed to be rocked to my core, have the sense knocked back into me or be hit in the face with a dumbbell in order to make serious changes.

So I quit my job, deleted his number, cut up my credit cards and checked myself in for shoulder surgery. While lying in the hospital bed post-surgery, dipping in and out of a panic attack because the nerve blocker they'd put in my arm was making me feel like I was down one limb, I thought of yogi Dan and chose to focus on nothing but my breath.

Life changed dramatically after this. It was the wake-up I needed. Each dislocation correlated with me putting all my energy into the wrong things; this was too blindingly obvious to ignore. The wasted energy was literally manifesting itself physically in my body. It was time to rewrite the script.

So there I was, consciously concentrating on feeling the good feels, thinking the good thoughts and convincing myself I'd cracked the manifestation code, but there was a nagging voice in the back of my head that didn't believe manifesting what I wanted was possible. I questioned everything. I felt completely unsupported, and I didn't feel worthy of the things I was trying to create.

This is when the faith part of the Manifestation Equation began to bloom for me. I grew up with a non-practising Jew for a father and a non-practising Catholic mother. I attended a private Catholic girls school but was excused from participating in any religious practices that made me feel 'uncomfortable'. I professed to be an atheist who didn't believe in God, but the truth was I *did* believe in something, it just didn't really have a name.

My mother had grown up facing a similar predicament. Aside from a period in her early teens when she had convinced herself that she wanted to become a nun, Catholicism hadn't sat well with her. Yet she still believed in a higher orchestration. We used the term 'the universe' a lot at home, even though I don't think I quite grasped the enormity of the concept. It was such an ingrained part of our vernacular that I didn't think it odd to use it in regular conversation until the girls at my Catholic school started looking at me like I was a kook.

Like many teenagers, I struggled with organised religion as a whole. It felt restrictive, fear-based, burdened in tradition and incredibly outdated. Yet there was also a part of me that felt as though I was missing out by not being a part of a religion. I recall several arguments with my mother during which I demanded an explanation for why neither parent thought me worthy of being assigned a religion at birth. So I bestowed the religion of no religion on myself and stuck a big neon 'ATHEIST' label on my chest.

For a girl who professed to not believe in the existence of God (the very definition of atheist), there were parts of my Catholic-school life I loved. Going to chapel was one of the highlights of my week, although I kept this to myself—it was so not cool to say out loud. The routine of chapel brought with it a sense of inner peace and calm, although I couldn't attribute those feelings to anything specific, it was just an overwhelming sensation that I found myself developing a taste for. I loved the stained-glass windows, the ritual, the sermons and the concept that there is a force greater than us that is always looking out for us. The girls at school referred to this force as God, and it wasn't until my mid-twenties that I felt comfortable shedding the atheist label and fully embracing this same force as the universe.

Like many young people, I felt that the world was against me. The shoulder dislocations, the broken foot, the toxic relationship, the narcissistic boss ... these were all down to bad luck or, even worse, bad karma; they were just my lot in life. But when I began to realise that my thoughts and feelings were having a profound effect on the things that were 'happening to me', it dawned on me that perhaps the world or the universe wasn't against me at all. It was, in fact, working in my favour and only had my highest interests in mind.

That simple shift in mindset cemented the faith part of the Manifestation Equation. Not only was it necessary to believe in a force much greater than myself that only had good intentions for me, but it was also essential for me to believe that I was worthy and deserving of the very best, always.

So for the next few years, I tried the Manifestation Equation version 1: thoughts + feelings + faith = successful manifestation. Think the good thoughts, feel the good feels, trust in the universe and bask in the glory of my manifestations. But still, there was a gaping hole.

Sure, sometimes things worked in my favour and finding prime parking spots would be a breeze, or I'd manifest a run-in or a phone call with a specific person. But the big stuff—the money, the soulmate, the ideal clients and those business opportunities—still eluded me.

Of course they did! I was missing the last essential ingredient of the equation: action. How arrogant of me to think I could just conjure up my dream life by sitting on my ass, thinking about my future, feeling as if I were already in my future and trusting that it was just going to show up one day. NO! It doesn't work like that.

YOU are the integral piece of the Manifestation Equation. The degree to which this equation is successful for you comes down to the actions that you're willing to take to make that dream future a reality. When you can take action with your thoughts in the right place, your feelings aligned with high vibration and complete faith that the universe is supporting you wholeheartedly, then you, my friend, are well on your way to a pretty awesome existence.

I said it before and I'll say it again (in case you chose to ignore me the first time), the Manifestation Equation is not a magic spell or mystical mantra—it is a self-empowerment tool that, when used correctly, can and will change your life. It can be used to attract almost anything to you, as I'll explain in detail in Part Two: The Practice. For now, just know that the equation remains unchanged no matter what you're trying to manifest.

CHAPTER 2

What's Stopping You from Manifesting?

Since entering the workforce at the age of twenty-one, I've landed dream job after dream job. My belief systems around my self-worth in the workplace have always been incredibly strong. My parents echoed my sentiments, colleagues always loved me and, like the Little Engine that Could, I had confidence that I could get where I needed to go in my career. Whenever I'd land one of these dream jobs, I'd hear comments like, 'You are so lucky!' Or, 'You must know the right people' and, 'You've got the gift of the gab!' And while elements of each of these things are true, the larger truth is I've been manifesting dream jobs my whole life, whether I was conscious of it or not, because, just like that little engine, I've never doubted that I could.

But when it came to the belief systems I held around my love life, I wasn't as lucky. My self-worth in that department had been trampled on from the age of nineteen, and for years I struggled to manifest a healthy love in my life. In my early days of experimenting with manifestation, a dream man was high on my priority list, but the universe kept bringing me men who met me at the limits I'd placed on myself when it came to my belief of what I deserved.

There was Beau, the 'love of my life', my 'soulmate' who was tortured by his fear of commitment, denial of his feelings and his own self-worth issues. I spent more than five years in that relationship, and then four years after that emotionally stuck on the relationship and unable to move on because, on some level, I didn't believe I deserved more.

Then there was Earl, the handsome knight in shining armour who defended my honour by yelling at a bunch of kids on the bus when I'd broken my foot and was standing propped up only by my oversized moon boot. He made them give me a seat, but it turned out Earl was the kind of guy who liked yelling, and not just at kids on the bus but at everyone: waiters in restaurants, people driving a kilometre below the speed limit and, eventually, me. He was also an emotional replica of the boss I had at the time. The victim role I placed myself in at work eventually became the role I assumed at home with him.

Then there was Callum, a poster boy for the 'dream man'. He loved me from afar for three years and became perfectly unattainable when his job sent him abroad. This relationship was all about *my* fear of commitment and about being in a relationship without actually *being* in a relationship. Nailed it.

And, not to sound like a total hussy, but there were also a few more in the mix over the years: the boring-as-all-hell guy, who entered my life when I had no passion for … anything; the alcoholic who hid his addiction from me (or did I choose to ignore it?); the cheater whose tastes ran to the 'ladies of the night' variety; and then there were also three whole years where I was unable to manifest a man of any description!

I recount my romantic (or lack thereof) past not to have my *Sex and the City* moment, but because this string of failed relationships is a wonderful example of how our limiting beliefs can become massive roadblocks when it comes to manifesting what we want in our life.

Which area of your life always feels a little harder than the others? Finances? Career? Or perhaps you, too, struggle with love. If you don't believe that you're worthy, deserving or simply that you can do or have what you want, then it's impossible to master manifestation in the areas where you feel limited.

IDENTIFYING YOUR LIMITING BELIEFS

We all have them. Some are more ingrained in us than others. A belief is simply a series of thoughts we have over and over again until we take it as gospel. But where do these thoughts come from and how do we overcome them?

Beliefs can stem from our parents telling us something is so in our childhood, and they can come from our cultural background, organised religion, the education system, friends, the media and even the barista at your local coffee shop if you're particularly impressionable. And, if you allow me to dip my toe in a 'woo-woo' reference, your limiting beliefs may even come from a past life (I know, how do we stand a chance?). The reason these beliefs manage to set up a permanent camp in our frontal lobe is because we never question them.

Limiting beliefs are not the same as bias. They will attach to you without conscious thought and they will bury their way into your psyche, going unnoticed until all of a sudden you realise there is a block in your life and it all leads back to this one thing that you've been telling yourself on repeat for god knows how long.

They are called limiting beliefs because they do exactly that—they limit us by creating unnecessary boundaries and self-built blockades that prevent us from accessing the things we've convinced ourselves are out of reach. They also happen to be wrapped up tightly in intense emotion, and, as you'll discover in Chapter 4, emotions are full of vibrations. And according to the Law of Vibration, we are magnets for things vibrating on a similar frequency to us. If you believe that you'll always be in financial debt and you feel fear around money, then you will attract more of those fear-based lack vibrations into your life.

And here's the crazy thing about limiting beliefs: most of the time they're false! But once that belief is set, we filter out evidence to the contrary, including the perfect relationship, ideal job and comfortable pay cheque. I filtered out Mr Right because he didn't match the subconscious limiting belief I held about what sort of man I deserved.

Uncovering limiting beliefs is a process I return to again and again throughout my manifestation practice. It's also the very first thing I encourage people to do when they keep hitting a proverbial brick wall with their manifesting. Russian playwright Anton Chekhov said, 'Man is what he believes.' When those beliefs empower, encourage and motivate us, our potential is infinite, but when we believe we are small, unworthy or undeserving ... well, our lives reflect just that. This is why understanding your limiting beliefs so you can begin to question and change them is so important, especially when it comes to understanding manifestation and particularly the Manifestation Equation.

Humans have the innate capacity to create, and whether we're doing it consciously, unconsciously or subconsciously, we are constantly manifesting and thereby creating our own realities. What the Manifestation Equation allows you to do is manifest consciously with intention by allowing you to identify your limiting beliefs and replace them with *limitless* beliefs. Sound good?

In Part Two of this book, I'll walk you through how to apply the Manifestation Equation to all areas of your life, and you'll hear me referencing limiting beliefs over and over again because I can say with absolute conviction that they are the number-one thing stopping you from manifesting. But there's also something else preventing you from epic manifestation, and this one triggers people more than the fact that their own beliefs have been preventing them from realising their dreams. What is it, you ask? I'm preparing you with this suspenseful lead-up because you'll probably feel the same heart pang I felt when I first discovered it.

IT'S JUST NOT YOUR TIME
(AKA IT'S JUST NOT MEANT TO BE!)

I mean, really. How demoralising! You work on your self-worth, you tell yourself you are deserving and then it's just 'not your time'? Give me a break! But the more I work with the Manifestation Equation, the more it becomes crystal clear to me that sometimes we just can't see the bigger picture. The parameters we set ourselves are marked with specific timeframes, human impatience and experiential expectation, and it is in these instances that our faith is truly tested.

Perhaps that thing you're so desperately trying to manifest is not ready to be manifested yet; perhaps it will never be ready! Maybe it's not the thing that is in your highest interest. If you feel like you've missed out on something or an opportunity has passed you by, it's probably because something so much more rewarding is on the way.

Does this bring you comfort? I hope it does. 'This or something better' has become the mantra that gets me through the darkest of days. Because even when you get this manifestation thing down pat, and even when you earn yourself the title of Manifestation Queen (or King), you'll still hit bumps in the road. I'm telling you this truth at the beginning of this book because I want you to believe me when I also tell you that this equation works, I'm just being honest about the challenges you will likely face.

Shit's gonna get real in the pages of this book. I'm going to tell you things you're not going to want to hear, and if you do the work, you'll uncover things about yourself and your belief systems that may just surprise you—and not necessarily in that delightful way you get surprised when you open the door to a flower delivery.

This type of work is called 'shadow work'. It describes going into the darkness and having a look at the parts of yourself that make you uncomfortable. Past teachings of manifestation have tended to dance around and avoid this shadow work. And while I'm not here to make you face your demons, I'm not going to sugar-coat the work it's going to take to master manifestation. But if you weren't ready, you wouldn't have picked up this book. You're already taking action—go, you!

If you've tried manifestation in the past and failed, I'm here to be your cheerleader and encourage you not to give up! You've never tried it like this. The Manifestation Equation covers all bases. All I ask is that you're honest, open and kind to yourself as you devour the pages of this book.

CHAPTER 3

Thoughts

Remember that film with Mel Gibson and Helen Hunt where Gibson's character electrocutes himself in the bathtub with a hair dryer (or something equally as idiotic) and then acquires the ability to hear what women think? An intriguing gift, no?

While there's probably a part of you that is dying to know what your partner really thinks of your mother, or what runs through your boss's mind when you negotiate for that pay rise, the reality of having such a superpower would be absolutely terrifying. Imagine if we could hear each other's thoughts, or, even worse, if people could hear yours?

I've already had several unsavoury thoughts since waking up this morning (which, for your reference, was barely two hours ago). I've also had a bunch of thoughts that were untrue, nonsensical, fantastical, self-deprecating and, well, a little judgey if I'm being completely honest. And I daren't say I am alone. Even the most Positive Polly feels safe having a negative internal reaction, and perhaps this is our downfall when it comes to the nonsense that goes on in our head. No one else has access. It's our own private free-for-all. It's a space where we can have an opinion without a reaction or consequence. But are your thoughts really free from consequence?

Yes and no.

THERE'S MORE TO THIS THAN
JUST THINKING A THOUGHT

It has come to my attention that this area—the power of our thoughts on manifestation—is where the distinction has not been made clear in past manifestation teachings. Your thoughts (BUT not ALL of your thoughts) are incredibly powerful, and when used correctly they do have the ability to shape your reality. But it requires a hell of a lot more than just thinking the thoughts for the manifestation to happen. Which is kind of a relief.

I am a pragmatist (hopefully you'll learn to love this about me) and, as I said in Chapter 1, I am a big fan of the teaching of the Law of Attraction, which states that **positive thoughts create a positive outcome, and negative thoughts create a negative outcome**, but I just can't ('and I won't!' she says as she dramatically stamps her foot, and shakes her fists in protest) get on board with the notion that all you need to do to manifest something is think about what you want to create and *poof* it's created! I find that idea almost as scary as Mel Gibson being privy to my internal dialogue.

But in the past, this is exactly how a bunch of people wasted their efforts when it came to trying to successfully manifest. Somewhere along the line, things got a little muddied around the practicalities of manifestation. Call it the Hollywood effect, mass marketing or an epic game of Chinese Whispers, but somehow the expansive, grand and intricate concept of manifestation got boiled down to this: thoughts become things.

And all of a sudden, a bunch of people were under the impression that simply thinking about the million-dollar mansion they were going to live in or the navy blue Maserati with white leather interior that they'd be driving one day, while not thinking about their unpaid bills, would be enough to manifest a big fat cheque. Unfortunately, all that came of this simplistic approach was a lot of very disappointed people terrified to think a negative thought lest it come true, but not really any better off.

And I was not immune. Call me naive (or twenty-two years old), but I most certainly caught the 'thoughts become things' hype. I definitely gave this technique a good innings. Not only because there was momentum building around the concept from self-help books, movies and celebrity endorsements, but also because it seemed to work ... to a degree. As a former chronic overthinker (perhaps the best lab rat for such a concept), I could very easily get myself into a tight tangle of anxiety and insecurity over situations that I had pretty much made up in my head. This is the curse of the overanxious: a quick decline from thinking sensible, present and mindful thoughts to fearful, catastrophic and essentially fabricated future predictions.

Anyone who has suffered from or experienced anxiety can attest to the fact that the bad things we worry about so viscerally hardly ever end up manifesting. But unfortunately, on the rare occasions that they do, you remember them and they form an imprint and an excuse as to why you need to be so worried, stressed, fearful or agitated all the time.

So I tried this 'thoughts become things' concept on for size. Perhaps all my worrying could be replaced by looking at the situation (or impending doom, as it usually was) with a little more positivity. This approach certainly worked when it came to my personal relationships. Instead of convincing myself that my boyfriend was cheating on me when he met a female friend for lunch, left to go fishing in the wee hours of the morning, didn't answer my calls while he was at work or (insert any other ridiculous, normal, everyday activity here), I chose to focus on what I knew to be true about our relationship—that we were madly in love. And, just like that, our relationship actually improved (I know, crazy!).

There was also that time I went for a job interview and decided to focus only on what my first day in my new role would be like rather than on how I'd prevent myself from crying when they told me I was the worst candidate they'd ever seen, and that I would need to think about ways of selling my organs on the black market because nobody in their right mind would ever hire me. (No judgment please! We've all had overly dramatic, unrealistic and highly unsubstantiated thoughts. It's what makes us human.)

Surprise, surprise, the interview went well and I got the job. Sure, we can get better at pulling ourselves back from the edge by practising mindfulness and staying in the present moment, but you mustn't think you're failing if unsatisfactory thoughts creep in.

Thinking positively impacts us exponentially. When I started to look at things in a more positive light, I learned that it was safe to think the best of a situation. It was okay to believe I was worthy of a desirable result. Expecting the worst wouldn't necessarily soften the blow of disappointment.

But did thinking positive thoughts make me a millionaire? No! Did not thinking about paying my electricity bill make it disappear? No! Did my electricity get cut when I didn't pay the bill? You can bet your last dollar it did. Because although thinking good thoughts made me feel better and the ripple effect of that was definitely an improvement on how I felt when I thought the world was against me, it didn't make manifesting specific things any easier. And this isn't because thoughts aren't capable of shaping our reality, but rather because thoughts require a little more juice before they can manifest. So let me share a few cold, hard truths about thoughts!

THOUGHTS ALONE ARE MEANINGLESS

And by this I don't mean that they don't matter, I just mean that even if you attached meaning to every single thought that passed through your brain, very few of these thoughts would make any sense to anyone but you. Our thoughts make up our internal world—a world that nobody else has access to (not even Mel Gibson).

Think of the billions of people on this planet. Inside each person's head are thoughts that make up their internal reality. But outside of that, outside of their thoughts, there is only one REAL world. Sure, we are each at the centre of our own reality, but if thoughts were really that powerful, the one world that we all live in would be way more complicated than it already is. Each one of us would regularly be collateral damage in another person's negative, pessimistic thoughts come to life. The fact that we aren't means our thoughts are real only to us, except for the fact that the majority of our thoughts aren't even real. And this brings me to the next cold, hard truth …

The majority of our thoughts aren't even true

I'm too fat. I don't deserve that. I'll never get that job. I'll never meet another man like him. I'll always be poor. I can't run a marathon … Any of these sound familiar? If so, not only are they not true, they are also just the thoughts you're having about yourself. What about all the (untrue) thoughts you're having about other people? She gets everything she wants. He's just lucky. They're the perfect couple. She's prettier/ more successful/happier than me.

While it's hard to gather definitive and conclusive evidence when it comes to our thoughts, research from Michigan State University suggests that we have anywhere between 50,000 and 80,000 thoughts running through our heads a day, and roughly 80 per cent of these thoughts aren't even true! That's a lot of unnecessary crap spinning through our heads. Here's another hard truth that will blow your mind ...

We're having the same thoughts over and over again

According to that same Michigan State University study, 90 per cent of our thoughts are repeats of thoughts we had yesterday, and the day before, and the day before that! Which, to me, indicates that we really shouldn't give them too much weight. We think them because we've already thought them, and before we know it those repeated thoughts pile on top of each other until one day ... BAM! You've formed a belief around them!

YET, THOUGHTS ARE POWERFUL

I want to be super clear that I am in no way trying to prove that our thoughts are not powerful or suggest that our thoughts aren't a key tool for manifestation, because they absolutely are. I just want you to understand that on their own, they mean diddly squat. Take comfort from this: thinking something doesn't make it so.

So how do we power up our thoughts and use them wisely? Let's start by looking at how thoughts can work against us. Earlier, I touched on my misguided manifestation journey and the series of unfortunate events that led me to develop the Manifestation Equation. My recurring thoughts of things never working in my favour resulted in just that, disappointment after disappointment. Here's an example.

I organised a trip to Bali with three girlfriends for my thirtieth birthday. At the time, I was working in a miserable job that I was dying to quit and I desperately needed time away to take a few breaths. In the lead-up to the trip, I started to tell myself it wasn't going to happen. Even though the tickets and accommodation were booked, my leave had been approved at work, the skies were clear and we were good to go, I was still overwhelmed by thoughts that we weren't going to make it to Bali—they consumed me. I felt heightened anxiety and fear around this trip, and I truly believed in every cell of my body that we weren't going to get on that plane.

The day before our flight, the Sangeang Api volcano in Indonesia violently erupted and a giant ash cloud began its descent over Denpasar. A total of thirty-one flights were cancelled, and ours was one of them. Flights did not start up again for another five days, but because hundreds of people had been on those cancelled flights, we couldn't get on another flight for eleven days. I went back to work with my tail between my legs.

Did my thoughts create a volcanic eruption in Indonesia? No. But there's no denying that a reality manifested in the exact way I had envisaged because I had placed all of my energy behind it. I've already articulated that most of our thoughts aren't true, and on some level we know this. Even though we might say, 'I could never lose the weight', the reality is that we know this is not a definitively impossible task. Similarly, if you think it's inconceivable that you'll ever finish writing a book (I may or may not be speaking from personal experience), deep down you also know that it's absolutely possible that you can finish (I did).

But when we believe wholeheartedly without a doubt that something is true, well, then that's when our thoughts start to gain a little bit of momentum. Take the placebo effect, a medical theory that works on the premise that the brain can trick the body into healing if it believes something to be true, i.e. when a patient feels better after being administered a fake drug that they believe to be the real medicine.

The placebo effect isn't limited to medicine. A good friend of mine was preparing for an important job interview scheduled for the following day when he received a phone call from his girlfriend, who ended their relationship. Eeep! Tim was understandably rattled by this news, and instead of continuing to prepare for his very important job interview, he begged me to meet him down at the pub for a relationship post-mortem. I begrudgingly agreed, and offered to buy the drinks that afternoon. I knew alcohol wasn't the answer to Tim's problem, and I also knew that he'd regret it big time if he got drunk before his interview, so, unbeknown to Tim, I quietly asked the bartender to hold the vodka from the vodka, lime and sodas I ordered that night. Three soda waters in, Tim started to act a little tipsy. Five soda waters in, he suggested we flag down a cab and get ourselves to bed. I didn't tell Tim about my deceit for a few weeks. 'But I felt drunk!' he exclaimed when I finally revealed the effects of the placebo. Our thoughts are powerful convincers. Your job is to determine which thoughts are true and which ones aren't.

While there is no conclusive evidence behind what causes the placebo effect to work, researchers believe it's because of a complex neurobiological reaction that increases feel-good neurotransmitters, such as endorphins and dopamine, and causes greater activity in certain brain regions linked to moods, emotional reactions and self-awareness.

Tip

I suggest purchasing a journal that feels really special to you, and I'm personally all about the writing implement, so a nice pen, too, if you're into that kind of thing.

Exercise 1
OBSERVING YOUR THOUGHTS

Observe your thoughts over a 24-hour period. Notice when your thoughts are unsubstantiated and untrue, and when they are true and can be proven without a doubt. Question the thoughts you believe to be an absolute truth, and determine whether they are or if you just think that they are true based on your own perception and/or what you think you're capable of. You can use a journal to keep track of the thoughts if you like.

This leads us to the fuel that thoughts thrive on: emotions. Our thoughts become supercharged when we add feeling to them. When we place an emotion behind a thought, it brings it to life and ignites neurotransmitters in the brain that send messages to our body's major systems and kickstart the process of taking it from a simple thought to a physical manifestation.

In his book *Breaking the Habit of Being Yourself*, Dr Joe Dispenza speaks of the thinking and feeling loop:

> *As you think different thoughts, your brain circuits fire in corresponding sequences, patterns and combinations, which then produce levels of mind equal to those thoughts.*

Put simply, the brain produces specific chemicals when you think different thoughts so that you are essentially able to feel what you're thinking. So when you think happy thoughts you feel happy, and when you think fearful thoughts you feel fear.

Think about this completely unrealistic (for most of us) scenario of being caught in the middle of a jungle with a ravenous tiger. The thought most likely to race through your head is, 'Ooh! That tiger looks hungry, I should probably run.' This thought alone isn't going to save your life. In fact, the thought is meaningless. But the emotion of fear that you place behind the thought is what sends messages to your nervous system—sending you into fight or flight mode and pumping you full of adrenaline in the process. This is what (might) save you from being tiger feed. What will really save you is taking action and RUNNING! Because thoughts aren't real until we act on them.

You can think about building that dream house, going on that European holiday, paying off your credit card, or leaving your job and working from your local café, but until you make it happen, none of it is real.

So yes, thinking the good thoughts is an integral part of manifestation, but unless you give them conscious awareness, place feeling behind them, act on them and believe them wholeheartedly to be true, they aren't likely to become anything more than just some of the 50,000+ thoughts floating through your head, day in and day out.

Now that you know what fuels your thoughts (awareness, emotion, action and belief), you can start to see how the Manifestation Equation works and why thoughts are the very first part of it.

Thoughts become the origin of your intention, and intentions are how we begin our manifestation practice.

What are intentions?

When attempting manifestation, it's important that you're clear on what you want to start creating in your life. For this reason, I believe a well-rounded manifestation practice starts out with a clear intention.

Intentions often get confused with goals or wishes, so I think it's important we make a distinction between the three from the beginning.

GOALS

A goal focuses on future achievements and is often task- and outcome-orientated. It can only have one of two results: success or failure. And while it's helpful to have things to aim for, it's important not to get bogged down in timeframes, logistics, practicalities or analysis. Setting goals is a cognitive exercise that can often be planned to the nth degree, often leaving no room for life to get in the way.

WISHES

'I wish I was taller.' I say this every time I meet up with some unusually tall girlfriends I went to high school with, or when I'm around my sister, who is taller than the average Levin. I got seriously screwed in the tall-genes department, but wishing to be taller is an unattainable and fanciful notion. It's never going to happen. NEVER!

The phrasing of 'I wish' sets a certain tone of hope and longing for a future that we aren't in control of and for something we believe is out of reach ... even if it's not. Think about the contexts in which you wish for things: I wish I had more money. I wish I could meet somebody special. I wish Ryan Gosling would leave Eva Mendes and knock on my front door one Sunday morning and be like, 'Hey Girl.' ... You get it.

Wishing is something you do on a star. It takes you and your ability to make choices out of the equation. It relinquishes the action piece.

INTENTIONS

An intention is something you practise in each and every moment. It's about enjoying the journey as much as the destination. It doesn't have a specific timeframe, checklist or pass/fail conclusion. It's mindful, fluid and open to change, and built on values and feelings. I like to think of an intention as a way to direct your energy.

The fluidity of an intention is perhaps its most redeeming quality. It's not rigid or bound by parameters. It's yours for as long as you need, and you're free to release it without a feeling of incompletion or failure when it no longer feels right for you.

How to set intentions

All intentions have to start somewhere. Thoughts are the origin of an intention, which is why I introduced you to thoughts right at the beginning of the Manifestation Equation. And, just like your thoughts, intentions come to life when you attach feeling, conscious action and a little bit of faith to them.

Throughout the next four chapters, we're going to be developing and building upon a set of intentions so you can see the full impact that your intentions have and how each component of the equation builds upon the other.

You're here to manifest the future of your dreams! So what does that future look like? Have you taken some time to think about what you truly want to create in your life?

I like to kickstart the process with a simple free-writing exercise (see opposite page).

FOUR POINTERS TO HELP YOU WITH INTENTION SETTING

1. **Try not to set more than five intentions at a time.**

   If we have too many intentions, they begin to lose their power.

2. Language is key with the three Ps:

★ **PRESENT:** This can feel super weird at first, but intentions are most powerful when we write them in the present tense.

For example, rather than writing 'I want to be a successful published author', you would write 'I *am* a successful published author'.

Good intention starters are 'I am', 'I have' or 'I feel'.

Exercise 2
FREE-WRITING

You'll need your journal, a pen and a timer. Set a timer for 10 minutes. Write a heartfelt letter to your present-day self from your future self, outlining all of the wonderful things you have in your life. This future self could be you one year from now, five years from now or twenty-five years from now . . . whatever resonates with you.

My letter might go something like this:

> Dearest Jords,
> What an incredible life we have created! I'm just back from my interview with Oprah Winfrey, she interviewed me for part of her SuperSoul Conversations—she's just as endearing and charismatic as we'd always hoped she'd be!

You get the idea. The trick to free-writing is to keep writing until the timer goes off. Don't pause, don't edit, don't judge and try not to think too much. The beauty of this exercise is that it pulls stuff from your subconscious mind that might not necessarily come out if you were to take the time to stop and think about it. And THINK BIG! Nobody but you is going to read this.

★ **POSITIVE:** I've already highlighted the power of thinking positively, and the same applies to writing your intentions. Keep it positive. Rather than writing 'I no longer have toxic relationships in my life', write 'I am in a loving, respectful and joyful relationship'.

★ **POTENT:** Nobody wants to hear you waffle, especially the universe, so when writing your intentions keep them short and sharp. Get to the point in one or two sentences—any longer, and the intention begins to lose its potency.

3. Don't worry about specifics

How is this intention going to manifest? When is it going to happen? Where is it going to happen? Why would it possibly happen to me? You don't need to worry about any of these things. As soon as we try to answer the how, when, where and why, we start to set parameters for our intention and we narrow the ways in which it can manifest. Some of my best manifestations have come in ways I could never have imagined!

For months I wrote 'I have $20,000 in my bank account' in my intentions journal. I came up with this number after calculating my credit card, student loan and other debts. As a small-business owner who did a lot of freelance work, my income stream was variable, but there wasn't a job I could dream up that would bring me $20,000 in one lump sum, mainly because this had never happened to me before. But still, I stuck with the intention and attempted not to work out the how, when, where or why. Even though past experience had shown me it probably wasn't possible, I couldn't say for sure that it was absolutely impossible.

Out of the blue, I received an email from a woman I'd met a few months earlier at an intimate work event (which I almost didn't go to). She wanted to know if I was interested in a big project she was putting together. This job was absolutely in my skill set and well within my capabilities, but I'd never done such a thing in this particular capacity before. In fact, I didn't even know a role like it existed. Having never done this specific job before, when she asked me to send her a quote for the job, I calculated as sensibly as I could and then pretty much pulled the rest out of my arse (the plight of the freelancer). She came back the next day with a sincere email that said, 'I'm afraid you've severely underquoted for this role, and we'd feel more comfortable paying you $20,000. How does that sound?'

If I'd been too specific when setting my intention, outlining where the money was going to come from, how it would appear and when I would receive it, I would have set too many parameters. I could never have dreamed up the way in which the scenario played out.

Did I spend that $20,000 paying off my debts? No. But we'll get to that later.

4. You can't set an intention for someone else

Dang! I know. It's so unfair! We'll explore why this is in Chapter 7, but for now just know that you can't set an intention for anyone else, or set an intention to change someone else (trust me, I've tried both).

Exercise 3
EXTRACTING YOUR INTENTIONS

Now that you've read through the pointers about setting intentions and are clear on those, it's time to re-read your free-writing from Exercise 2.

What desires came up for you during the free-writing exercise? Was it what you expected? Quite often, when I do this exercise, I uncover desires I didn't even know I had. It's a great starting point for intention setting.

Using your free-writing as a guide, extract five intentions that you want to work with over the next four chapters of this book. Write these down in your journal, keeping the three P's from pages 55–6 in mind as you do.

SO, WHAT HAVE WE LEARNED?

★ We've learned that thoughts are an integral part of the Manifestation Equation, BUT thoughts alone are meaningless.

★ We've also learned that the majority of our thoughts are untrue and are simply repeats of thoughts we've had the day before.

★ We also know that thoughts become powerful when we place emotion behind them, when we take action towards them and when we believe them to be true.

★ Thoughts are the origin of our intentions, and they are the place where the manifestation begins to form.

★ Thoughts kick off our creative process, daring us to dream bigger than we can conceive for ourselves.

★ But, perhaps most importantly, thoughts also shape our mindset. And although a positive mindset alone isn't enough to manifest the things you desire, without it, manifestation will escape you.

★ Thinking positively improves self-worth, reminds us that we deserve the very best and allows us to expand and grow rather than shrink by telling ourselves we aren't capable.

★ And I think we can all agree that expecting the worst definitely does not cushion a fall, soften the blow of disappointment or protect the heart (or ego).

★ So watch your thoughts, but don't judge them. Know that, at the end of the day, you have a choice about whether they become 'things' or not.

CHAPTER 4

Feelings

If thoughts are the origin of our intentions, then feelings are the origin of our vibrations. And an intention doesn't gain momentum until we can tap into how manifesting that intention will make us feel.

In the same way that the power of thoughts is often attributed to the Law of Attraction, the power of feelings can be attributed to another universal law known as the Law of Vibration.

I know you're not meant to choose favourites (or perhaps that only applies to children and pets), but the Law of Vibration is my favourite of all the universal laws. Like most things, this law can be as complicated or as simple as you like, depending on how deep you dive into it, but, at its most basic level and for the purpose of understanding its role in the Manifestation Equation, let's keep things simple.

The Law of Vibration states that **everything in the universe vibrates on its own frequency, and that things with a similar frequency are drawn together.**

And when this law says everything has its own vibration, it means everything! You, me, the trees, rocks, cars, books, bacteria, illness, planets, that horrendous vase gifted to you by Aunt Doris, that fly on the wall, EVERYTHING. It doesn't matter if it is a living and breathing organism or an inanimate object.

You know when you just 'vibe' with someone? This isn't just an expression thrown around by hippies; vibing is a real thing that happens when your vibration is on a similar frequency to someone else's. Conversation flows, you feel like yourself around them, and they make you feel safe, free and like the best version of you. The same goes for when you just don't vibe with someone. On paper you should be the best of friends, but something indescribable just *feels* off.

I have a love/hate relationship with dating apps. You can't read someone's vibrations through a smartphone (trust me, I've tried). It doesn't matter how great their selfie game is or how articulate their bio is (probs written by their sister), there is no way of telling if you'll have a real connection without meeting that person in the flesh.

I recall this one guy I met on Bumble. On the app, we were a perfect match. I found him très attractive in his photos, his messenger game was strong—he was funny, articulate, engaging and the perfect amount of curious. We arranged to meet for lunch the following day. The minute I sat down and we had our first five minutes of face-to-face interaction, I wanted to leave. Not because he didn't look like his profile pics, because he did. Not because he wasn't the man he described in the app, because he was, and not because he was shy or awkward or had nothing interesting to say. It was because we just didn't vibe. The energy was off.

Now most of you (my friends included) would say, 'Geez, Jord! Give the guy a break. He was probably nervous', but I've been on enough dates to know that when you know *you know*. And I know you know what I'm talking about.

Because when the vibration is bang-on and the chemistry between you is electric, indescribable and show-stopping, you just feel it! And the person you feel this with could be the opposite of what you thought your type was. We'll dive deeper into the vibrations of chemistry in Chapter 11, but chemistry is a relatable example of vibrational frequencies. And this isn't limited to romantic chemistry. You can also feel chemistry with friends, work colleagues and strangers on the bus. I often feel it with baristas, but perhaps that says more about my coffee addiction than vibrational frequencies. (Side note: coffee and I are definitely vibing.)

Another great way to explain vibrations is when you pull an oracle or tarot card out of the deck and you're like, 'Holy moly this really resonates with me!' Well, that's because the card is vibrating on the same frequency as you. You're drawn to it, and it's drawn to you. Another example of vibrations in action is when you randomly pick a book off the shelf, and it's the perfect book for you in that moment in your life. Coincidence? Nope. Same freakin' frequency! Pretty cool, huh?

Finding this a little hard to get your head around? It's probably because vibrations (or energy) are not something we can see, touch, hear, smell or taste. In other words, our sensory system is completely oblivious to them, therefore it's easy to believe them to be false or unproven, especially when it comes to inanimate objects.

Although a wooden chair might look solid, within that chair are millions and millions of subatomic particles that are vibrating at a particular frequency. Because you can't see them with the naked eye, it's easy to discount their existence, but that doesn't make them any less real.

Take a dog whistle. We know for a fact, thanks to science, that dogs can detect sounds that humans can't hear. Even though none of our senses can pick up the sound vibration of that whistle, a dog's can, so we believe it to be real.

If you take the dog out of the equation, does this mean that the sound no longer exists? No. And the same goes for the Law of Vibration. Just because there is no quantifiable proof of its existence doesn't make it an untruth. In fact, once you start working with it, it's impossible not to believe in its existence.

According to the Law of Vibration, when it comes to manifesting what we want in our lives, we need to start vibrating on a similar frequency to the things we're trying to attract. But how does one do that?

Well, let's start by looking at energy and the different ways we're already shifting it when we feel stuck or low. Whether you're a yogi, a runner or a professional booty shaker, you know the mood-boosting, energy shifting, high-vibe tonic that is moving your bod! When energy feels stuck or stagnant, I always tell people to JUST MOVE. You can do it sitting at your desk if you have to. Vigorously shake your hands, fervently stomp your feet, power walk up and down the corridors, do squats in the kitchenette while you're waiting for the kettle to boil. It doesn't matter what it is—just get energy moving through your body.

Whenever I can't shake a 'mood' (and, as a Gemini, that can be a little more often than I'd like), I do as T. Swift instructs and I 'Shake it off'. Do it now. Stand up wherever you are and convulse your body like you've been electrocuted (I recommend doing this in the privacy of your own home, as this attracts too much attention in public spaces) or, if you've got some actual rhythm, break out some booty-shaking dance moves.

On a biological level, when you move, the neurotransmitter dopamine is released into the body, and you start to feel 'better' and full of new energy (or vibrations). On an emotional level, when you move, emotions have the opportunity to move through you, and sometimes this might mean they manifest unexpectedly. Have you ever been sideswiped by a sudden onset of tears in savasana? Or overcome by anger when you hit a stride in your afternoon run and start pounding the pavement like your life depends on it? That's because simply by moving you've provoked a vibrational shift, and emotions that have been ignored, suppressed or simply bypassed are being stirred up and pushed to the surface. When the shock of an unprovoked emotional release occurs, there is often this sweet relief and sense of euphoria that follows. The human body was made to move, and moving it with conscious awareness moves stuck and stagnant energy and keeps us vibrating on a high frequency. This goes for life's problems, too. As great as stillness is, and there is absolutely a place for it, often just moving is enough to impact a situation into growth so it progresses into something more (or into decay, if it has reached its natural conclusion).

And what about music? You're feeling flat, perhaps a little sad and kind of lethargic. You're meeting friends in half an hour and you think, 'How am I going to get myself out of this funk?' You reluctantly shower and put on a Spotify playlist titled 'Get me the F out of this funk', and before you know it a beat kicks in, your foot starts tapping on the tiles, your booty starts shaking in the spray of the shower and you're belting out Pharrell Williams like it's nobody's business. Instantly you feel like you could conquer the world (in your bath towel); you're feeling excited, sexy and full of energy. This, my friends, is a vibrational shift, and music is a master at it.

Music can lift your mood in an instant, or do the opposite. My friend Zelda would lock herself in her room for days after a break-up, alternating between two albums—Taylor Swift's *Red* and Joni Mitchell's *Blue*—until all the tears inside of her were out. At the time, I felt she was being overly dramatic, but in hindsight I see she was doing herself a world of good by feeling her feelings and shifting her vibrations.

How do you feel when you clean the house or rearrange your furniture? Is it an instant energy booster? The Chinese philosophy of feng shui is built around the idea that energy plays a vital role in the placement of objects and the cleanliness and minimalism of your home. Personally, I know that when my house is clean and my room is clutter-free, I sleep better and generally feel happier than when I'm drowning in a sea of lightly worn yoga pants and sweatshirts that aren't dirty enough to wash yet but aren't quite clean enough to put back in the drawer. The same goes for watching a feel-good movie, catching up with close friends or savouring a glass of red wine after a long day. You can feel things shift on a cellular level.

The common thread through all of these shifts in vibrations comes down to how they make us feel. By tapping into and bringing conscious awareness to our feelings, we can make significant changes to our vibrational frequency and our manifestation practice.

Feeling the feels

Here's the thing about feelings: most of us are *thinking* our feelings rather than *feeling* them. This means we're not using them to their highest potential. Perhaps it's Western culture (which admittedly I have seen a definite shift occurring in), but feeling too much has been frowned upon/looked down on throughout history as a sign of weakness and fragility. But the truth is that when we don't feel our feelings and instead choose to ignore or suppress them, they manifest in other areas of our life, often showing up as confrontations, lessons or physical symptoms and even illness.

So, how do we feel our feelings?

LET'S STOP CATEGORISING OUR FEELINGS AS 'GOOD' OR 'BAD'

All feelings are equal, legitimate and vibrationally charged. Some are high vibrational feelings while others are low vibrational feelings, but they all need to be felt and are just as valid as each other.

Low vibrational feelings like fear, grief, shame, dread, hate, guilt, jealousy, insecurity, anger, worry, doubt or disappointment are feelings that we often avoid at all costs. And while it's true that if we stay in these feelings unnecessarily we can invite in negative events (cue the dislocated shoulders, cancelled holidays and relationship meltdowns), running away from them won't make them disappear, it will only make them manifest in the most dramatic of ways.

Exhibit A (or are we up to E by now?)

I was working in a horrible job. And by horrible I don't mean lame, boring or unsatisfactory. On paper, it was a dream job, but I was miserable. I was being bullied and overworked by a narcissistic boss, and the side effects of this were becoming evident in almost every area of my life: another relationship had been ruined, most of my friendships were suffering and my health was not in good shape—I'd put on six kilos in the first six months of working there, I'd had the flu for what felt like a year, and I had zero energy to do anything outside of work or communicate with anyone. Worst of all, I felt trapped by the status of my job and the highly coveted position I found myself in. If there had been a physical way to measure my vibrational scale from 1 to 100, 100 being enlightened and 1 being despair, I would have been sitting at negative 1.

My days were full of dread, fear, anxiety and overwhelm. I was defensive, fatigued and highly irrational. I also happened to be highly obsessed with my eating regime at this time and so meal prep had become a top priority for me, even if that meant preparing breakfast and lunch for the following day at 11 pm when I should have been unwinding or sleeping.

One night, after a giant day at work, I was in the middle of my usual late-night manic rush to get everything ready for the next day. I was finishing off an article that was due at 7.30 am the following morning with one hand while texting a colleague about said article with the other hand. I had some quinoa cooking on the stove, I was roasting sweet potato in the oven, and I also had a load of washing running in the laundry room of my apartment building that needed to go into the dryer before bed. I pressed save on the article, send on the text, let the sweet potato do its thing, turned the quinoa down to simmer and raced down (in the dark) to the laundry to transfer the clothes to the dryer. On my way to the laundry, I slipped on some junk mail lying innocently in my path.

Everything moved in slow motion as I descended towards the tiles. While most people might stretch their hands out to catch themselves as they fell, I was too terrified to put out my arms (hello history of dislocated shoulders). I held my arms tight against my chest, and the only left thing left to cushion my head from smashing into the hard ceramic tiles was my right foot.

The pain was horrendous, but it was also the kind of pain you experience after stubbing your toe on the coffee table—it felt like death and certain amputation, but I was convinced that within a few minutes it would fade. So I limped down the hall to put my clothes in the dryer (priorities) and made it back just in time to save the quinoa from turning to mush. Win!

I rang my mum. She said it was imperative that I ice and elevate my foot pronto for at least a couple of hours. But it was now 10.30 pm and I had to be at work in less than 8 hours, so I slapped an icepack on it for 20 minutes, popped a couple of anti-inflammatories, did one last edit of the article and then went to bed.

When my alarm woke me at 6 am, all I could feel was a throbbing sensation coming from my foot. It was so intense that I was surprised to not see the doona pulsating. I tentatively pulled the covers back and caught sight of a swollen limb that kinda resembled my right foot, but thanks to the red, black and various shades of purple it looked more like it belonged to something from an 1980s horror flick. I should have been worried, but that article needed to be posted, and I wondered if my clothes were dry. Had I remembered to get the sweet potato out of the oven last night? I hobbled to the bathroom (hmm, definitely not going to be able to wear closed-toe shoes to the office today), then sent a photo of the foot to Mum to get her opinion on whether it warranted forking out for a taxi fare that morning.

'JORDANNA!' (Mum only uses my full name when I'm in trouble, being ridiculous or out of my god damn mind.) 'You have to get to the doctor right now!' Don't be silly, I thought, there's no doctor near work. But as I tried to get dressed, I realised there was no way I was getting out my front door alive, so I texted the pic of my foot to my general manager and worked from the couch.

I stayed on that couch for four days, except to get to the bathroom and to bed. By day four, my foot was blacker and even more swollen, so I decided it was time to seek professional advice. I went to the physio who pulled a serious I've seen this before face, but I could tell he was appalled and shocked. 'You HAVE to get an x-ray immediately. That foot is broken,' he said in a calm yet somewhat alarmed voice.

'Broken? Absolutely not! I don't have time to have a broken foot. I barely have time to cry from the pain of said foot, kind sir. Please give me some cream and crutches, and I'll be on my way.'

Next thing I knew, I was getting an x-ray, being told I had a fracture from my pinky toe to my ankle, and being fitted with a moon boot. I stumbled around on crutches for six weeks after that. Two of those I enjoyed from the comfort of my own apartment. It was incredible how much more work I got done when I didn't have a dragon breathing fire down my neck or telling me I wasn't good enough, fast enough, smart enough or dedicated enough. It was revealing and liberating to have a little bit of space to allow all of those feelings I had been suppressing for months to bubble to the surface and actually be felt, and subsequently released.

When I returned to work not much had changed, but I spoke up more when I was being spoken down to. I felt physically powerless (because moon boot) but tried my darndest not to feel emotionally, psychologically or mentally powerless. It was hard! Too hard. And it took me one more injury (or was it two?) to finally hand in my resignation and abort, abort, abort!

If you're constantly operating from a place of high anxiety, dread, fear and insecurity (which I was, 24/7), your body, the universe and probs most of the people around you are telling you to get the hell out of there! And if you ignore the symptoms (which are essentially what feelings are), then the lessons are often forced upon you and will manifest as injuries, accidents or an illness. The broken foot was just one of many physical manifestations of the toxicity of that job, and if I hadn't gotten out when I did, I don't feel I'm being overly dramatic in saying the next manifestation would have been far more serious and had a greater long-term effect on my mental health.

Low vibrational feelings don't necessarily mean the frequency of those feelings is low or undetectable. In fact, the frequency of them might be blaring and they can, and will, attract situations and people of a similar frequency into your life. Low vibrations feel dense, heavy and physically draining.

In contrast, high vibrational feelings such as happiness, joy, enthusiasm, freedom, love, passion, belief, gratitude, abundance and enlightenment are also operating at an exceptionally high frequency but feel lighter, expansive, clear and calm. There is a definite distinction between the two, but both are just as powerful when it comes to manifestation.

When trying to manifest and shift our vibrations to feelings of joy, happiness and love, the goal is not to ignore, suppress or avoid low vibrations, because that, my friends, is damn near impossible not to mention unrealistic.

All feelings are valid, and all feelings should be felt. But your job, as you begin to master manifestation, is to work out—just like you did with your thoughts—what feelings are true and necessary, what feelings you have the power to shift and upgrade, and whether you're truly feeling them or just thinking them. In every moment you have the choice to feel anything you want, whether the current situation reflects that or not.

For example, when you feel doubt about a certain situation, can you instead choose to feel curious and see if there is more to discover? Or, if you feel anxious about a situation, can you choose to feel peace about it until there is proof that you need to be feeling otherwise?

Ignorance or the unknown is the fuel for so many low vibrational feelings. We feel anxious because we're unsure of the future, or fear because we can't see what lies in the shadows, but instead of operating on a lack of information, look at what you know for sure, and feel into all of the feelings you have stored deep inside of you.

There is a meditation that I take my clients and event attendees through all the time called the High Vibrations Meditation (the link to this is on page 337 if you want to download it). I ask them to feel a certain feeling in different areas of their body, from their heart to their eyelashes, from their lungs to the backs of their knees.

This meditation is a really effective way to truly start to embody feelings. Because when you can embody a feeling, its vibrational nature of constant movement will either attract something of a similar frequency towards you or give you an opportunity to release it. You've probably heard the saying 'emotions are energy in motion', and they absolutely are. This means that when we take the time to feel emotions (good or bad) and really drop into them, we either connect with them and shift our vibration or we allow them to move the vibration through us.

If you don't allow yourself to feel fear by either avoiding it or keeping it as a thought pattern in your head, you'll just keep pushing it down and suppressing it, and it will continue to manifest in different parts of your life. But if you can feel into the fear and familiarise yourself with it, it will either dissipate completely or morph into a new feeling like relief, safety or love. Make sense?

CREATING THE SPACE TO FEEL OUR FEELINGS

I can already hear you saying, 'Who has time to feel fear? I'd rather just suppress it.' Oh, I hear you! But it doesn't work like that, which my broken foot scenario demonstrated. If you don't allow yourself to feel a low vibrational feeling such as fear, it will just manifest somewhere else. The same goes for high vibrational feelings. If you don't make time to feel happy, how on earth do you think you're going to attract more happiness into your life?

You have all the time in the world to feel busy, tired and bored, and if you want to feel high vibrational feelings such as love, joy and freedom, you'd better hope there's some space to feel them when they arrive.

What if you took 10 minutes every day to sit in stillness and tap into the feelings that you want to bring into your life? Really *feel* into happiness. How does it feel in your throat, belly and scalp? How does it feel in your left hand, on the sole of your right foot or on your lips? If you're vibrating with a high frequency of happiness, what kind of things do you think you'll be able to attract? Vibrations are powerful. Make space for them, and use them wisely.

LEARN HOW TO CONTAIN YOUR FEELINGS

Let me be clear, containing your feelings isn't the same as suppressing your feelings. In order to fill up our cup, we need to be FILLING UP

OUR CUP! If you host a party and fill up everyone's glass with expensive champagne, you'll soon discover that there isn't much left for you to enjoy. And by this I mean it's all very well feeling the feelings, but we don't want them leaking out of us like a running tap—we should be filling up on and absorbing their vibrations. So sure, be kind to others, but first show kindness to yourself. Be generous, abundant and give love, but first find those vibrations within you. Because if you're constantly creating these vibrations then handing them out like free candy, you're missing out on a tonne of the benefits. And I promise you this: once you contain your energy and fill up your own cup, you'll find there is PLENTY to go around.

TAP INTO A REMEMBRANCE OF THE FEELING

A lot of people ask me how they're meant to feel into a feeling they've never experienced before. I truly believe that we have access to every single feeling within the spectrum of human emotion; they're all contained deep inside of us. You have an innate ability to tap into every single emotion required to manifest anything you want. And don't underestimate the ability of your imagination. Here are a few tricks I like to use to help people tap into certain feelings.

Trying to manifest love but don't feel you've ever truly been in love? You must have experienced the vibrations of love at some point. Love for a family member, a pet, an experience or even a movie, so feel into that. Another one of my favourite ways to tap into the vibration of love is to watch a really cheesy rom-com, not a tragic love story, but something that makes you love the idea of love.

Trying to manifest financial freedom but feel like you're drowning in debt and can't see how you and money are ever going to be friends? Can you recall a time that your money situation was different? How did that feeling compare to what you're feeling now? OR What other feelings would financial freedom allow? Stability, assurance, peace, relief … Can you tap into those feelings?

Perhaps you're familiar with stability in terms of relationships. You can tap into the same peace you feel after a yin yoga class. How did relief feel in your body that time you were running to catch that flight and you made it to the gate with 30 seconds to spare? All of those past vibrations are still stored deep inside of you. You just need to remember them and then start vibrating on their frequency by feeling them.

Bringing awareness to your own vibrations grants you the ability to alter, expand and attract the vibrations around you. It's how psychics predict people's futures. What they're actually doing is interpreting your energy and vibrations to see what direction they're headed. This means that if you can learn to shift your vibrations, you can direct your energy towards a future outcome that you desire. This, my friends, is manifestation!

Now that we know how feelings impact our vibrations and how our vibrations impact manifestation, let's start to incorporate feelings into our intentions.

Feeling your intentions

We have already established that thoughts are the origin of an intention, and that feelings are the fuel required to fuel a thought, so it's imperative whenever you set an intention that you attach a feeling to it. For example:

I am in a loving, respectful and exclusive relationship (this is the intention). It makes me feel joyful, free and safe (these are the feelings attached to the intention).

OR

I have a successful and popular book on The New York Times *Best Sellers list (this is the intention). It makes me feel accomplished, abundant and proud (the feelings attached to this intention).*

Once you can place a feeling behind your intention, it gives the intention a vibrational frequency. And, in the same way that you write the intention in the present tense as if it is already true, you also need to start feeling those feelings as if you're already experiencing them.

Exercise 4
ATTACHING FEELINGS TO YOUR INTENTIONS

Grab your journal and go through the five intentions that you created in Exercise 3. Now attach at least one feeling to each intention. How would having that intention manifest make you feel?

Once each intention is vibrationally charged with feeling, your job is to feel into those feelings as often as possible. You can do this in many different ways. I like to incorporate it into my daily meditation practice, but you don't have to meditate to master this. Simply set aside some time daily (or weekly, if that's all you can manage) to feel the sensation of already having manifested your intentions.

This part is non-negotiable. If you can't connect with the feeling of already having your intention, then you're going to find it difficult to attract that intention towards you.

SO, WHAT HAVE WE LEARNED?

★ The Law of Vibration states that everything in the universe is vibrationally charged and that feelings are our tool for shifting and manipulating those vibrations.

★ If you want to attract something into your life, you need to start vibrating on a similar frequency to it.

★ When you don't vibe with someone, it's because your vibrational frequencies are not aligned.

★ Most of us are *thinking* our feelings rather than *feeling* them.

★ There are no good or bad feelings; they are all valid and necessary. However, you can choose which feelings you want to stay in and which feelings just need to be felt and released.

★ Watch feelings that leak out of you like a running tap, and learn to contain your feelings so that they can influence your vibration.

★ If you're trying to manifest a certain situation, tap into a remembrance of the feeling attached to it. If you can't remember or access that specific feeling, think of some other feelings that would result from manifesting that same intention, and tap into those instead.

★ Intentions come to life when you fuel them with feeling. Until you place a feeling and vibration behind an intention, it's just a thought.

CHAPTER 5

Actions

I like to call this the 'Bitch, please' chapter. Get ready for some tough lovin', because I'm about to deliver. We've looked at our thoughts and their potential power when used correctly. We've covered feelings and how essential they are when setting intentions and shifting our vibrations to align with what we want to create in our lives. Now it's time to move into the real nitty gritty of manifestation: the co-creation piece.

The action and faith elements of the Manifestation Equation go hand in hand. Just as thoughts and feelings make a dynamite team, you and the universe also play an integral role in manifestation when you work together.

It's funny, when I first started teaching this equation, I thought the part of the equation that people would find the easiest would be the action component. After all, it's the only part of the equation you have complete control over, and as a self-confessed control freak, I find that incredibly appealing.

But most people struggle with action and say things like, 'You mean I have to actually take steps towards what I want? Can't I just think about my soulmate and write down their ideal traits?' And there's also the classic, 'But I've been feeling like the right job will just come my way.' Well, yeah it might. But when was the last time you searched for job vacancies? Have you sent your CV to your ideal companies? Have you updated your LinkedIn profile lately? Do you even know what kind of job you'd like?

This is a self-empowerment book above all else, and the action that you take in your life is the very definition of empowerment. For too long the action part of the puzzle has either been left out of the majority of manifestation teachings or has been given far less weight.

Esther Hicks writes, 'While action is an important component in the physical world in which you are focused, it is not through your action that you are creating your physical experience.'

These words kept me stuck for so long. Because I'm sorry, but we *are* creating our physical experiences through our actions. Like most humans looking to get out of taking responsibility for their own life, I relinquished the action component. I felt like I had been given permission to just keep thinking the thoughts and feeling the feels. This thought pattern, whether you have read the work of Hicks including *The Law of Attraction* or not, is a get-out-of-doing-the-work card. And if you've already tried to practise manifestation, this is most likely why your past attempts have failed. While surrender and non-attachment are vital components of manifestation, and there will be moments where action is *not* required (I'll address those in the next chapter), more often than not it is the part that YOU play that not only guarantees momentum but also allows you to sit back after the fact and say, 'I totally made that happen.'

OWN YOUR FUTURE AND THE ROLE THAT YOU PLAY IN CREATING IT

Empowering yourself begins with taking ownership for everything that happens in your life. I said it earlier, but it bears repeating: things are not happening *to* you, *you* are making them happen—the good, the bad and the ugly. I have spent a long time mulling this over to make sure I've looked at it from all angles, because I get it: innocent people experience tragedy, loss, trauma and heartache all the time. And while some schools of thought will not make an exception for these incidences, saying instead that those individuals are responsible for attracting ALL of it, my view is not as rigid. While it is true that negative things can happen when we give too much awareness, attention and energy to things we are so desperate not to attract, it's simply not fair to say that a defenceless child who has been subjected to abuse is responsible for what happened to them.

But I'm not talking about the defenceless and the innocent. I'm talking about the situations that happen in your life that you immediately relinquish responsibility for, pass blame on for and take no ownership of. The lover you never meet (because you're buried in your work). The promotion you never get (because you've never asked your boss). The money you can never save (because you've never written a budget). The business success you don't have (because you aren't acting on your 'big idea').

Enter the Law of Action. Even the non-woo-woo, least open-minded and most practical among us can get on board with this universal law, which states that **you must do the things and perform the actions necessary to achieve what you are setting out to do**. Manifestation is the recognition that *you* play an integral role in creating *your* future! It's as simple as that, folks.

In order to manifest anything successfully, the Law of Attraction and the Law of Vibration require the Law of Action. I mean of course they do, right! It baffles me that this simple, relatable and totally understandable law gets pushed to the side. If you're serious about manifestation, you have got to be willing to take action. Sure, the thoughts, the feelings and the faith help big time, but without the bit where you actually do the things, your life just comes down to luck and chance. And I don't know about you, but I don't like the sound of that at all. I want to be confident in my old age that when I look back on my wonderful life I will be able to say, 'I created that. I made that happen.'

For a very long time, I left action out of my manifesting efforts. I thought positively, I felt all of my feelings and I had an exceptional (some might say exemplary) spiritual practice. But then I waited. And waited. And when my knight in shining armour didn't drive up in my brand new car, carrying a briefcase of $100 notes and my book-publishing deal, I assumed I just wasn't thinking positively enough, or that I hadn't been feeling it enough. Or was it that I didn't believe in it enough?

Woe is me! Nothing good ever happens for me. I'm just unlucky. I can't ever get ahead.

I'm pretty sure I've uttered all of these statements more than once, and you'll be forgiven if you have, too. Too often it can feel like life is happening to us, and that we don't have control over our destiny. BUT WE DO! If no one has ever told you that, consider this your wake-up call. You always have a choice and can do anything you want to do. Sure, you might not be the best at something, you might not succeed, heck, you might even experience pain, but don't ever think you're not the creator of your future. Whether you take the action or not, something is being manifested, so wouldn't you rather it was being manifested with conscious awareness?

You may have heard the quote, 'Things don't happen to you, they happen for you.' I think it was originally penned by American author Byron Katie, but it hit home for me when Jim Carrey used it in a commencement speech he gave to graduates in Iowa in 2014 (it's always the celebs and their viral YouTube clips that get all the credit). You may not *always* be creating the situation, or bringing people and obstacles into your life, but perhaps they are being put in your path for you, to allow you to learn, grow and expand. Let that sink in. The things that perhaps were not caused by your actions happen for you, so that you can take action and assert responsibility for whatever happens next.

Responsibility is your ability to respond! So how are you going to respond when things don't go your way? Are you going to allow yourself to get steamrolled, or are you going to pick yourself up and move out of the goddamn way?

Remember that narcissistic boss I had? Annabel wasn't my first bad boss. In fact, I had worked for versions of Annabel throughout my entire publishing career. They got incrementally worse the higher I climbed up the corporate ladder, and each one prepared me in some way to tackle the next in line. I couldn't see that at the time, of course. But on reflection it was super clear that with each boss came a lesson, and I could choose to act upon, learn from and grow from that lesson, or I could choose to play the victim.

Class is in session

When I was eighteen, I worked as a legal secretary at a criminal law firm. My boss, Babs, was a criminal lawyer, a champion chain-smoker and notoriously ruthless (I guess that's what made her a good solicitor). She always had a Vogue cigarette in one hand, a red pen in the other and a scowl on her face. She yelled at me constantly, not because I was doing anything wrong but because she yelled at everybody. According to the other secretaries in the office, she actually liked me more than any of her previous employees, but she had a funny way of showing it. Perhaps it was a bit like that boy in primary school who teases you because he fancies you. I spent most days crying in the bathroom or whining on the phone to my boyfriend, who would pick me up every afternoon and listen to me bitch and moan the whole way home.

'Well, why don't you say something to her?' he would mutter under his breath. 'Stand up for yourself, Jord. And if you can't do that, leave! You deserve better *AND* I don't want to hear about it anymore.' (That last bit was less muttering, more yelling.) I had never asserted myself against anyone, let alone a middle-aged criminal lawyer who paid me minimum wage and spoke to me like a deaf poodle.

I decided I couldn't stand up to Babs, so I chose to resign. I took responsibility for the situation by taking action and leaving, but that wasn't quite the lesson I needed to learn ...

Fast-forward five years, and I was twenty-three and working full-time in publishing as an editorial coordinator. My boss was a wonderful female editor. She was in her sixties and was a hip grandma type who treated me like a granddaughter. She was nurturing, encouraging and a wonderful mentor. Unexpectedly, I was given a promotion by the general manager and was swiftly moved from coordinator to junior writer and marketing assistant. This new role meant I now had two bosses: Hip Granny and the marketing manager. These two women were not friends. In fact, I quickly became the child between two bickering divorced parents. Hip Granny turned on me and made every day at work torture. So now here I was, crying in a new bathroom cubicle and being reprimanded for enduring such bullying by a new boyfriend (who was less compassionate than the first). The difference between Hip Granny and chain-smoking Babs was that I actually liked this new job and didn't want to leave it, so I gathered the courage to stand up for myself and make a formal complaint to my general manager, who took the matter to HR. I thought I'd finally broken the pattern of nasty female bosses, but it turned out I was just getting started ...

I moved out of that frying pan and into the fire of a new job where I worked under an editor-in-chief who didn't appreciate my swift rise from the bottom of the food chain to assistant food editor in less than nine months. She did her best to tell me how hopeless I was at my job every chance she got. After her came the 'celebrity' food queen who felt threatened by a younger up-and-comer. She encouraged my exit from publishing to explore the world by not renewing my contract. Shortly after that came a manager with a split personality who waved a pair of kitchen scissors at me when I pointed out a mistake she had made in a recipe. Thanks to each job, I got stronger, wiser and spent less time crying and more time working harder in order to not let these women deter me from my path. I felt like the protagonist in a video game, defeating the monster at the end of each level, but with my smarts and self-worth rather than a sword. I wasn't aware of it at the time, but all of these women were preparing me for my final battle—the ultimate test of my ability to stand up for myself and not be bullied. This lesson took me longer than I had anticipated, and was taught by the most challenging boss of them all, Annabel.

I tell you these stories because they are an example of what we can create in our life for our own future benefit. At any point during those life lessons I could have played the victim—in fact, I did several times— but I didn't play the victim long enough to stay stuck. Was I bringing those female bosses into my orbit? Damn straight! But not necessarily because my thoughts and feelings were attracting them (as some manifesting philosophies would have us believe), but because there was a bigger lesson for me to learn in life, and they were my classroom.

Can you see the difference?

On paper, there was a lot of evidence to say that I had 'bad luck' when it came to my employers OR that I was a terrible employee (after all, I *was* the common denominator). But instead of playing the victim, I took action. I took responsibility and created a pretty awesome career for myself, which I don't believe would have been possible without spending time in the trenches. This is not to say you can't be successful without being yelled at, bullied or threatened with a pair of kitchen scissors, but I do believe that those situations didn't happen *to* me, but rather *for* me. I was given an opportunity to learn, grow and become the bad-ass (not literally, I'm super lovely) Lady Boss I am today.

The manifestation of Jordanna Levin, author, manifestation mentor, yoga teacher and speaker, was a culmination of me taking action after action after action. Not luck, not timing and not positive thinking, but action!

The time I spent with Annabel was my moment to rise from the ashes like a phoenix rather than become the patient wrapped in bandages and third-degree burns. The action steps I took in my career weren't all made with conscious awareness. It's only in retrospect that I can see how proactive I was in shaping my own future. It's all very well having the gift of hindsight, but this book is about taking the initiative to create the life you want with conscious intent.

TAKE CONSCIOUS ACTION STEPS

There really is no secret formula when it comes to taking action. You just have to do it. My advice to everyone is to start small. And if that feels too big, then go smaller. There are times in your life when you need to play big, and this may not be one of them.

I have found that doing a miniscule something is ten times better than doing absolutely nothing because it feels too overwhelming, too scary or too risky.

Exercise 5
WHAT ACTION STEPS CAN
YOU TAKE TODAY?

Grab your journal and turn to your five intentions (which now have feelings behind them). For each intention, write down one action step that you can take today to move yourself one step closer. Not tomorrow and not next week, but today!

If the idea of taking action feels overwhelming, go smaller. This could just mean changing your mindset or thought patterns around taking action. For example, your intention might be: I am in a financially rewarding and fulfilling editorial role in the publishing industry. I feel proud, worthy and successful.

Your action step for TODAY might be: I will search for available editorial positions online.

Or it could be as simple as: I will start *believing* that I am worthy and capable of a financially rewarding and fulfilling role in the publishing industry.

Each week, address new action steps that you can take for your intention. Some weeks these steps will be big and bold, and some weeks they won't. That's okay! Remember that to shift your vibration, all you need to do is MOVE. Your action is kickstarting the energy into motion.

IDENTIFY WHERE YOU ARE
WASTING YOUR ENERGY

Some of the biggest action steps I've taken have been around changing where I direct my energy. As simple as it can be to bring positive things into your life with the right thoughts and feelings, it's just as easy (if not frustratingly easier) to keep bringing in the wrong vibes.

Are you vibrating in a way that is actively and negatively impacting or blocking you? What are you creating in your life due to your wasted energy output? Working in a toxic environment was bringing more and more toxicity into my life. Injuries, failed relationships, non-existent friendships and a deep sense of self-loathing. Work took up all of my energy because I allowed it to. It consumed me and infiltrated all of my vibrations, and you know how vibrations work, right? You vibrate on a certain frequency, and you will attract more of those vibrations towards you.

The same can be said for staying in a relationship past its expiration date, or for always seeing the glass half empty, or for getting caught up in the crossfire of negative conversation and gossip. Now don't get me wrong, I love a little bit of gossip (I really am the poster gal for Gemini stereotypes). A royal scandal or Hollywood engagement is like crack to me, but there is a very fine line between harmless, hot-off-the-press celebrity goss and an all-out bitchfest! And although I've learned to consciously pull back when I can feel myself sliding down a slippery bitchy slope, I am now very conscious of the people I surround myself with and how their pessimistic undertones, petty comments and personal insecurities impact my own vibrations.

You see this play out in the workplace a lot. Someone has a whinge about the boss, and then the next thing you know it's a free for all.

Suddenly your lunch hour, tea breaks and the commute home are filled with a constant stream of bitching and moaning. It sets a tone in the office and becomes the central focus of conversation, and in a way it builds a kinship among employees. But this is kinship based on low vibrations folks (no matter how true the gossip is), and low vibrations spread like the plague and align you with the type of negativity you're spending your entire day whinging about!

When I worked with Annabel (and all of her predecessors), I was so guilty of this! Because when work gets toxic and overwhelming, it helps to talk about it. But when every conversation centres on that toxicity, and your colleagues then want to talk to you about their experiences, and what happened to Trudy on Level 3, or poor Boris in accounts, it's very easy to become totally consumed by it. And oh, how we allow it to swallow us whole.

If you can identify with this situation, whether at work, at school pick-up, or with your girlfriends over a couple of wines, I encourage you to pull back a little and disengage. I'm not saying that you can't be supportive of your peers, but just be super clear about their experiences and your experiences. The same goes for friendships and other people's relationships (aka my favourite place to stick my large Levin nose!).

There's a great Polish proverb: Not my monkeys. Not my circus. For so long, I hid behind the label 'empath', and I wore the burden of other people's dramas like a badge of honour. 'I can't help it, I just feel for them,' I'd say. And I've got a good inkling that if you're reading this book, you might be an empath, too. But, as promised at the start of this chapter, I'm going to give you some tough love and say that allowing other people's vibrations to affect yours doesn't make you a better person. In fact, if anything it lowers your vibrational frequency. By disengaging, you're not being selfish—you're setting a vibrational standard. If it's not your mess, it's not worth the effect it will have on your own good vibes.

The same goes for people in your life who talk you out of your dreams, encourage your fears or who simply don't believe in you. If you're constantly surrounded by their energy, over time this will impact your energy, even if you think you're ignoring their words.

But you know who your own worst enemy is? You! Ain't no bitch bitchier than the one we unleash on ourselves. Watch how you speak to yourself and about yourself. Watch where you're wasting your energy with negative talk like I can't, I never or I shouldn't. Actively catch yourself and replace this type of language with positive statements like I can, I do and I will.

Once you really start to tune into your energy, which hopefully this book is encouraging you to do, you will naturally start to notice where it's being wasted. It's then up to you to actively change your energy output to align with your intentions and an overall sense of wellbeing and positivity.

CREATE SPACE FOR YOUR INTENTIONS TO SHOW UP

Sometimes action is about having a bit of a spring clean in order to tidy up your present circumstances. Often, when we're trying to manifest new things in our life, there's actually no room for them when they show up. You wouldn't order a new couch for your lounge room if you had nowhere to put it, would you? Well, the same applies to new jobs, new relationships and new opportunities. There has to be space for them once they arrive. Spaces are vital to manifestation, and sometimes all they need to be are those small transitional moments between action steps. Those transitions are just as important as the action itself.

You hear this in yoga all the time through phrases such as 'the journey is just as important as the destination' or 'don't rush from one pose to the next; enjoy the spaces between'. A space can quite literally translate to the moment between one relationship and the next, a week off between jobs or perhaps that scary nothingness between your last sale and your next one. It could refer to those times in your life when it's been a while since the last win, but you're not necessarily losing—times when business slows down, there are no social events on the calendar and you're just plain free.

I feel this sense of space big time right before I'm about to make an important decision and I'm considering my options. An idea has bloomed, there's no going back, but a decision needs to be made in order to move forward. How do *you* sit in this space?

The funny thing with space is that we CRAVE it. We say things like 'I wish I had more space to create'; 'If only I had some more space to myself'; 'Space would give me the opportunity to do so much more.' Do any of these sound familiar?

But the truth is we're all freaking terrified of space! Any time we have a fleeting moment of nothingness, we jam it full of stuff. Whenever I used to find a gap in my life, I'd immediately scramble around looking for something to plug it with: anything to fill the void. I feared nothingness and thought it defined me as empty, lazy or boring. This fear shows up in the form of thoughts, like the ones on the following page.

I've got the whole day free tomorrow, maybe I should see if my sister needs help with the kids.

OR

A client just cancelled and freed up my afternoon, I'd better see if another client wants that spot.

I was terrified of space because I was never taught how to navigate it. Those moments in between and those transitions have no manual. They're sticky and unfamiliar. We know how to be excited. We know how to be disappointed. But few of us know how to just *be*. But when we can give ourselves permission to sit in nothingness and to treat transitions as juicy opportunities for growth, then this is where the magic happens because space is our friend and the better you get at creating it, the more effortlessly your manifestations can integrate into your life. There is pure gold to be found in those in-between spaces, if you dare to explore them.

HOW CAN WE CREATE MORE SPACE?

Okay, so now we know space is good! And we know we need more of it, but how do we go about creating it? Well, first things first, clear out the deadwood. What unnecessary stuff are you expending your energy on? Which things in your life are taking up room? Because when we're working on manifestation with the intention of bringing new stuff into our lives, there'd better be room when it arrives—just like that couch, it has to fit somewhere.

For a long time, I tried to manifest things and was so disappointed when they didn't happen. Then one day, I realised I had no room for my soulmate, business success or book deal. If all the things I'd been trying to manifest had shown up, where the hell would I have put them?

So what's the alternative? Clear your calendar in the hope that your dreams turn up at your back door? Quit your job in the hope that a new job will appear? Not quite, but taking the time to consciously be present and refusing to waste energy on toxicity and meaningless stuff is a good start.

I bet you're familiar with this quote by Alexander Graham Bell: 'When one door closes, another opens'. But you're probably less familiar with the rest of that quote: '... but we often look so long and so regretfully upon the closed door that we do not see the one which has opened for us.'

My mate Graham Bell is talking about wasted energy, folks! To create new things and open doors, we need to be able to receive them and not waste our energy on the toxicity or closed door we're longing to leave behind.

Exercise 6
TIME TO CLEAR SOME SPACE

Go back and remind yourself of your five intentions so you can get clear on what it is you are trying to make room for in your life. Then read through the questions below, and write down the answers in your journal.

1. Where am I wasting my energy?

2. Which areas of my life are in direct opposition to the new stuff I'm longing to attract?

3. Where are the opportunities for me to be still, do nothing and just be?

GIVE YOURSELF THE GIFT OF NOTHINGNESS

Most of us are taught from a very young age that if we want something we have to work for it. Even as kids we work on a reward system: do A and you'll be gifted B. And I am aware that this chapter is all about taking action. But I really want you to understand what action means. It means taking ownership of your life, and sometimes that means doing nothing!

Often, when we choose to do nothing, we're labelled boring, uninspired, unmotivated or lazy. But every answer I've ever been proud of, any solution I've ever celebrated, has come from a place of stillness. To receive the gift of intuition and insight, one must stop, recalibrate and listen. It is in the choice to do nothing that we test our humanness and receive our guidance, but most of us are running from nothingness out of fear! So I invite you to actively search for the pockets of nothingness in your life. Locate them, celebrate them and then sit in them. Let them induce vulnerability, curiosity and potential.

SPIRITUAL SIDESTEPPING

I feel this chapter is a good place to address a modern ailment of the 'spiritually awakened' or self-help and personal-development era: spiritual sidestepping. This is my version of the term 'spiritual bypassing', which was coined in the 1980s by psychotherapist John Welwood. He used it to describe a person's 'tendency to use spiritual ideas and practices to sidestep or avoid facing unresolved emotional issues, psychological wounds, and unfinished developmental tasks.' Basically using self-development and spiritual practices to avoid doing 'the work'.

I think we're all guilty of this to varying degrees, and I'm going to go out on a limb here and say that many of the spiritual teachings around manifestation invite you to sidestep the action part of the equation by placing a spiritual veil over the concept.

And this isn't limited to the practice of manifestation. How many times have you read or quoted *The Power of Now* (or insert any popular self-help book here)? But how many times have you actually practised the concepts it explores?

Do you hide behind your kaftans, crystals, incense or tarot cards? These things are pretty and wonderful complementary tools, but they do not maketh a person spiritual. Do you journal, pull oracle cards and burn sage every full moon to release the things that are no longer serving you? Do you just write these things down, or do you actively release them from your life? Do you pass the blame onto others in an argument by using spiritual lingo—convincing yourself they're just deflecting their energy onto you, or that this is about them not you? Newsflash: sometimes it *is* about you!

Do you focus on the 'love and light' side of spirituality but avoid or deny the shadows, inner work and pain that come along with it? Do you use your 'gifts' to play the role of victim? Earlier, I used an example of how empaths often do this by wearing their personality type as a badge of honour and blaming their feelings on others.

Do you use your zodiac sign as an excuse for certain behaviours? I'm guilty of this already in this chapter by using my star sign to explain my penchant for gossip. Libras can't make decisions, Virgos are perfectionists, Leos hog the limelight, Taureans are stubborn, Capricorns are void of compassion … the list goes on and on, but you're not bound by these traits AT ALL, and using them as an excuse for behaving badly is considered spiritual sidestepping.

So, too, is blaming the moon/planets/stars/Trump government for your reactions and choices. Similar to using your horoscope, this tendency comes out of a fear and mistrust of ourselves and our internal compass. The energy of a full moon might feel powerful, but it has zero power over your personal choices.

Do you think the universe will always look out for you? Well, it will, to a degree, and we'll explore that in the next chapter, but if you live your life believing that the universe is looking out for you so you are free to do whatever you want, then you're opening yourself up to a certain level of danger and a misguided view of the physical world. This is essentially the ultimate spiritual sidestep because it relinquishes all responsibility to the universe.

I raise the issue of spiritual sidestepping not to take anything away from what you already practise, dismiss your spiritual endeavours to date or tell you that any of the things I've just mentioned don't mean diddly squat, but because I want you to understand that your actions, and taking responsibility and ownership of your future, is what is going to have you manifesting your dreams, like TODAY!

SO, WHAT HAVE WE LEARNED?

★ Just as thoughts and feelings make a dynamite team, the action and faith parts of the Manifestation Equation go hand in hand. But the universe won't work unless you do!
★ The Law of Action is perhaps the easiest to understand of all the universal laws, but unfortunately it is missing from many of the manifestation teachings. The Law of Attraction and the Law of Vibration only gain momentum in conscious manifestation when you work with the Law of Action.

★ Life is not happening *to* you, you are making it happen,
   or it is happening *for* you.

★ Can you take conscious action steps towards your intentions?
   Small steps are better than no steps.

★ Where are you wasting your energy? Wasting your energy
   on toxicity and low vibrations does not serve you. In fact,
   it may even harm you.

★ You need to have space in your life for when your manifestations
   arrive, otherwise where will you put them? Can you actively create
   space in your life?

★ Sometimes taking action means doing nothing at all.

★ Watch out for spiritual sidestepping. It's essential that you take
   responsibility for your choices and actions, and do the real work
   if you want your intentions to manifest.

CHAPTER 6

Faith

Faith and religion are not one and the same. I think it's important to make this distinction right at the beginning of this chapter because, for me, confusion between the two hindered my willingness to explore my own faith, and ultimately my ability to trust in something far greater than myself for many years.

I touched briefly on my history with religion at the start of this book—and also on my parents' decision not to bestow a religion on me due to the fact that both of them had rejected the religions in which they were raised.

Although I can't dump all of the world's religions into one big pile and make wild sweeping statements about those who have a religion and those who don't, I can point out the difference between organised religion and what I mean when I talk about faith in the context of the Manifestation Equation.

Excuse me, while I generalise for a minute (not to offend, but just to make a point): the major world religions are centuries old and steeped in history and tradition. They are often systematic, dogmatic and enigmatic (hands up if you started singing 'Greased Lightnin''). Religions are based on a system of beliefs adopted from a set of teachings passed down through generations and, ultimately, said in the name of something greater than us—be this a supreme being, a god or gods, a teacher or a prophet. The representatives of these religions speak on behalf of that higher entity, and we are there to listen. And while there are elements of religion that I believe we need more of in society—community, ritual and reverence—there are components of many of the world's main religions that measure our own validity in this world based on a set of external factors.

Even though I was raised with no religion, I attended a Catholic school and, as with all facets of education, I was eager to learn and absorb information no matter the context. I actually really enjoyed the Bible stories, but that's all they were to me—stories. I loved the story of Adam and Eve in the Garden of Eden, and I dug Jesus of Nazareth. He made a cool protagonist in The New Testament, but to my young mind he felt more like a character—more like Jon Snow, Lord Commander of the Night's Watch—rather than my Lord and Saviour Jesus Christ. Sure, his miracles were cool: water into wine (handy), healing the sick and injured (saintly), walking on water (got to be better for your feet than the firewalking Tony Robbins endorses), feeding thousands with only five loaves of bread (tell me your secrets, JC), but what I related to was the messages and the lessons in these stories. Those I liked. The storytelling element I got! I was not concerned with the legitimacy of the stories, or wanting to prove whether or not they were true. But then Jesus was horrifically crucified as the ultimate sacrifice for humankind to relieve them of their sins, and the Bible lost me!

Now I know I can't sum up religion with a story, and trust me I'm not trying to, but for me growing up, religion was a set of stories and a bunch of rules I had to abide by so that one day I would get into heaven. And that just didn't resonate with schoolgirl Jordanna at all. As a teenager, when I swanned about town calling myself an atheist, I thought that part of wearing that badge meant not having a sense of faith because I didn't believe in God or the Bible. And I felt like I was missing out. But faith from a psychological perspective is our drive to search for meaning, purpose and significance in life. It is based on our own personal belief systems and on having the confidence to trust and believe so deeply in ourselves, but also *know* that there is a force much greater than us always working in our favour.

All religion involves faith, but faith, unlike religion, is fluid. It is not ruled by a set of principles and guidelines, but rather by a set of personal values. When we feel deeply connected to these values, we feel limitless and transcendent.

In the context of manifestation, and in particular the Manifestation Equation, faith is an unwavering confidence that you are being fully supported by not only your own vibrations but also by vibrations outside of yourself. You might call it the universe (I will in the context of this book), God, Creator, Source or Freddie Prinze Jr! What you call it doesn't matter, but I personally believe that having an unwavering faith in yourself and a greater force produces one of the highest vibrational frequencies there is, which is why it is such a dynamite tool for manifestation.

When I look back at teenage Jord, floundering through Catholic-school life, not sure what or who to believe in, feeling deeply that she didn't resonate with the God being taught in Bible studies, but scared to believe in nothing, I want to wrap her tightly in my arms and say, 'Believe in yourself and the rest will follow.'

Only when we can deeply trust in our own intuitive knowing can we be prepared to believe in something as grand, as indescribable and as immeasurable as the universe.

In the years that I have been practising and teaching manifestation, I have found that faith is one of the hardest things to teach. An individual's ability to have a deep sense of faith depends on so many variables: their limiting beliefs, childhood, education, relationship history, self-esteem, cultural background and so much more.

So, as I have done for most of this book, I will share what worked for me in the hope that it will resonate with you, too. For so long I didn't trust in anything, thinking that it was safer to question everything and trust nothing and no one; hoping that this would lessen the blow of disappointment. Well, as we have already discovered by looking at our thoughts and feelings, this is rarely the case. If anything, by expecting disappointment we almost guarantee that we will receive it.

A cheating boyfriend in my youth made me question the whereabouts and loyalty of every boy I ever dated after him. I brought this baggage with me into each relationship, and it was the source of many an argument. In one total cringe-worthy moment, I recall one boyfriend buying me a book (bless him) titled *Jealousy and How to Overcome It*. But the book wasn't what I needed; what I needed was a little bit of faith in my own judgment and trust in the people who showed me that they could, indeed, be trusted.

We do this a lot. We experience something one time and then use that as a blueprint for all similar experiences going forward. Which is the point, isn't it? To learn our lesson and not make the same mistake again. Only in these cases, we take things to the extreme by never allowing ourselves to experience a different version of the situation, assuming it will play out in exactly the same way as before. But questioning the motives and intentions of others all of the time and assuming the worst of people makes for a very lonely life. Which brings me to my first lesson in trust.

Treat every experience as a new one

I now walk into relationships (romantic and otherwise) with an unquestionable trust that whatever I experience is for my own benefit. Sometimes it's soulful, passionate and joyful, sometimes it's someone looking you square in the eyes and telling you they don't find you physically attractive (we'll come back to this charming chap later). And yeah, sometimes it's the most immense heartbreak you've ever experienced. But I truly believe you're vibrationally ready for everything you experience. Trusting in this notion has helped me big time.

Remember when I spoke about life happening *for* you? Well, trust plays into this premise. Every individual experience is put in your path for you to benefit from, not for you to be punished, judged or disciplined. Learning this changed the faith game for me because it gave me a sense of empowerment. If something happened, it was because I was ready for it.

When we feel well equipped to handle any situation, we do just that— we handle it! And nothing builds confidence more than trusting in something and having that trust pay off. But, like anything, trust takes practise. And the ultimate way to practise trust, especially when it comes to trusting in the universe, is to observe how it works.

Universal cycles and The Law of Rhythm

The final universal law that the Manifestation Equation is based on is the Law of Rhythm, and it really is a beautiful way to understand faith and not only learn how to lean into it, but also understand the profound impact doing so will have on your manifestation practice.

The Law of Rhythm states that **all energy in the universe is like a pendulum. It ebbs and flows, waxes and wanes, rises and falls, grows and decays**. This pendulum energy is what establishes cycles, developmental stages and patterns of nature that can be seen throughout the universal landscape.

The wonderful thing about the Law of Rhythm is that you can see it in action all around you at all times.

THE LUNAR CYCLE

It has been discovered that humans have been using the lunar cycle to measure time since the Palaeolithic era. For centuries, our ancestors used the lunar cycles to plant and harvest crops, hunt and fish, predict the weather and tides, follow the seasons and track the reproductive cycle of women. Today, biodynamic farming is based on the phases of the moon. Farmers will often plant their crops by the new moon, taking advantage of its powerful ability to promote growth. (Just quietly, this works for both hair and nails. Snip them on a new moon, and the rate of rapid growth is increased. You're welcome!)

My introduction to manifestation actually came about through the lunar cycle. The cyclical nature of the moon, when followed correctly, gives serious momentum to the way you set intentions. There are moon phases that occur through a 29-day cycle, and there is an energetic predictability that can be felt and harnessed through each phase.

The new moon and the full moon (or the show ponies of the lunar cycle, as I like to call them) are the two major anchor points of these energies. The new moon kicks off a new lunar cycle and brings with it a fresh, yang-based proactive energy (see page 114 for more on this). This is a wonderful time to plant new seeds and ideas, start new projects and set intentions. I've been running a sell-out event series since 2016 around the new moon and its innate ability to bring momentum to intention setting and manifestation practice. The full moon occurs halfway through the lunar cycle, and it shifts the energy into a yin-based state (see page 114). Things start to slow down, the energy gets a little denser and heavier, and the energy is encouraging us to rest, reflect and release the things that are no longer serving us.

Every single month, without fail, you have an opportunity to lean into the energies of the lunar cycle. And when you do feel the energy slow down, harness it and lean into it knowing that a fresh wave of creativity and action-orientated energy is about to sweep through with the next new moon.

THE SEASONS

There is so much more to the seasons changing than the shifts in temperature and the leaves changing colours. Energetically, seasons ebb and flow in such a forceful way that it's impossible to not be affected by them. Plants sprout, bloom and decay with the seasons, animals migrate, hibernate, shed their coats or grow new skin as the cycles change, and humans are not immune to the effects, either. We hunker down in the winter, experience a sort of optimistic euphoria in spring and are drawn outside to be more active in the warmer months of summer.

Ayurveda, the ancient Indian medicinal system, and Chinese medicine both use the seasons as part of their medical practices, especially when it comes to energy levels. Together, the seasons balance each other out. The pendulum swing from winter to summer, and the seasons in-between make a whole. They form a full life. I love the predictability of the changing seasons and the feeling of recalibrating as our systems adjust to these changes.

THE ZODIAC

It's rare to meet a person who doesn't know what star sign they are (even if they don't know what their star sign says about them). But our astrological signs are actually an area of space, and the 12 x 30 degrees form a band around the earth (called the Zodiac Belt). The sun enters each astrological sign one after the other for an entire year, always starting in the sign of Aries and finishing in the sign of Pisces. This cycle is as old as the universe, and it happens each and every year until the sun has completed its revolution (even though the sun is a fixed star and doesn't move, astrology is read from Earth's perspective, just in case your science brain started spinning when I spoke of a moving sun). Every astrological year, the energies shift and change, and just as we have a birthday each year without fail (I'm less excited about this the older I get), the sun is doing a full rotation through the zodiac, too.

MENSTRUAL CYCLES

Every month, women have an opportunity to tune into the Law of Rhythm by tracking their own menstrual cycle. It's no coincidence that it is often linked to the lunar cycle. In her book *The Path of Practice*, Maya Tiwari draws a parallel between the fertility, power and nurturing spirit of females and the 'sacred substance of mother moon'.

'The ancients called the dark days of the moon "woman's moon" or "resting moon", linking a woman's physical, emotional and spiritual state to the lunar wheel.'

A regular and healthy menstrual cycle will go through four distinct phases each and every month: menstruation, the follicular phase (pre-ovulation), ovulation and the luteal phase (post-ovulation). This cycle is essentially preparing a woman for pregnancy. But it tells us so much more than that. There is a school of thought that teaches that within a woman's menstrual cycles are internal seasons, and these seasons can be used to moderate and understand how her energy will fluctuate throughout the month.

Menstruation = winter. It's a time to surrender and release. To slow down, let go and take adequate rest.

Pre-ovulation = spring. It's a time that we feel motivated and bursting with energy. This is a great time to create and get tasks completed.

Ovulation = summer. It's a time that you're full of energy but more likely to want to be around other people collaborating and creating together.

Post-ovulation = autumn. It's the time to hold yourself as disturbances and your inner critic start to take over.

By observing your own internal rhythms, you're able to trust that if you're feeling a certain way that it is impermanent and you, just like the rest of the universe, are in a constant state of flux.

LIFE CYCLES

Everything within the universe that is alive will experience a life cycle of birth, growth, decay, death and rebirth (depending on what you believe). This life cycle of living matter, however, also applies to things like relationships, interests, experiences, ideas, creative projects etc. Because of our inability to let go, we often try to intervene in this process by delaying death. But the natural order of the universe means that it will always seek to find balance, and sometimes this means putting lives, relationships and ideas to rest in order for new ones to bloom.

ENERGY BREAKDOWN: YIN AND YANG

I feel like you've got this whole Law of Rhythm thing down pat, so I'm going to take it one step further. Energetically, within each universal cycle, there is another rhythm occurring: yin and yang energy.

The yin and the yang are important principles of Taoism (pronounced dow-ism), and together they are believed to bring balance and harmony to life. They are two opposites that make a whole.

Yang energy is upward and outward. Characteristics of yang energy include action, radiance, heat, masculine, external, proactive, reactive, acting, producing, day, logical, mental, fast and extroverted.

Yin energy is downward and inward. Characteristics of yin energy include passivity, coolness, feminine, internal, being, resting, reflecting, softness, darkness, night, permissive, slow and introverted.

You can see this balanced yin and yang energy throughout all universal cycles. As the seasons progress, we move from the yang energy of summer into the slower yin seasons of autumn and winter. We then pick back up again in spring as we slowly move back into yang energy.

When the sun rises in the morning, we move from the yin of night and dawn into the yang energy of midday, and we slowly progress into a slower more yin phase by nightfall.

Tapping into all universal cycles allows us to surrender to that natural rhythm and take advantage of the moments within the cycle that promote growth and expansion as well as the moments that require inner reflection and surrender.

The duality of yin and yang also teaches us about trust. You see, many of us are scared to trust in the unknown. If we knew the outcome, we'd have no problem trusting that a decision is right or wrong, or that things would work out. True?

But when you start to observe that we are also governed by the Law of Rhythm, as EVERYTHING in the universe is, it gets easier to understand that the pendulum is always swinging. If a death is occurring, it's because a birth is inevitable.

A really easy way to understand this premise is through the breath.

The breath

Breath is the ultimate recognition of creation and a beautiful reflection of how we cope with the cyclical rhythms of life. The breath is our greatest indicator that we are indeed alive, and when we reach the end of our life our last breath will be our final contribution.

It is also our life force and how we gather and release energy. From a yogic perspective, the breath is broken down into inhalation, exhalation and retention (the pauses at the top and base of the breath). Try the breathing exercise in Exercise 7 below.

In his book *Light on Pranayama: The Definitive Guide to the Art of Breathing*, B.K.S. Iyengar describes the different parts of the breath and their energetic qualities.

The inhalation is described as 'the intake of cosmic energy by the individual for his growth and progress'. It is linked to our actions and is

Exercise 7
CONNECTING WITH YOUR LIFE FORCE

1. Breathe in for the count of four. (Inhalation)

2. Pause at the top of the breath for the count of four. (Retention)

3. Exhale for the count of four. (Exhalation)

4. Pause at the bottom of the breath for the count of four. (Retention)

Repeat these steps for ten rounds. Were there parts of the breath that you found more easeful than others? Were there parts that you struggled with?

essentially our life force, the inhalation distributing said life throughout the body.

For Iyengar, the exhalation is 'the outflow of the individual energy to unite with the cosmic energy'. The exhalation is where we are able to surrender the ego and just be with Self. It's the process by which the body and mind unite and dissolve into universal energy.

Iyengar describes the pause between the in and out breath and the pause between the out and in breath as Kumbhaka, which means a pot that can be full or empty. When we practise breath retentions, it is 'a withdrawal of the intellect from the organs of perception and action, to focus on the seat of consciousness'.

By focusing on the four parts of the breath and having an understanding of how Iyengar describes the energetic components of each part, you will be able to see how we can use the breath to trust in the Law of Rhythm and the ebbs and flows of life. To break it down:

1. The inhale breath is how we receive. Quite literally, we are receiving life in the form of oxygen.
2. The pause at the top is how we sit with our receptiveness. That point of retention is essentially the space between, which I covered in the previous chapter.
3. The exhale is how we give and also our state of surrender. We are giving carbon dioxide back to Mother Earth.
4. The pause at the bottom is how we sit with the act of giving before we're able to fill up and receive again. This can be a very tricky spot to get comfortable.

Now let's apply this principle to different energy forms.

Applying the rhythm of breath to money

1. The inhale represents receiving money.
2. The pause at the top represents how we hold
    on to or save money.
3. The exhale represents spending/giving money.
4. The pause at the bottom represents that moment
    before money comes back in again.

Let's break this example down even further by using my not-so-great relationship with money as an example.

1. I'm good with the inhale. You want to give me some money?
    I will take it, my friend. I'm getting better at asking for it, and I'll
    take a nice deep inhale breath sucking all that money in.
2. I'm not so good at the pause at the top of the breath.
    When I receive money, something inside me feels the need to
    spend it immediately (we'll address this in the manifesting money
    chapter). I move straight from the inhale to the exhale with no
    pause in the middle—I just want to spend those dollar, dollar
    bills, y'all!
3. Now, I don't think I'm alone when I say the pause at the bottom
    is probably the hardest bit of the full breath cycle. When you're
    low on cash, can you trust that money is just another energetic
    cycle and that it is guaranteed to flow back in again? Can you
    use the breath (a constant and effortless cycle) to remind
    you of this? Just as the inhale is inevitable after an exhale, it is
    also inevitable that after we spend (or give) money, it will flow
    back in again (receive).

Realising this changed EVERYTHING for me! I'm going to go as far as to say that I significantly reduced the majority of the anxiety I had been experiencing my whole life, not just around money, but around everything. Relationships, creative projects, business sales, EVERYTHING! Because no matter how bad things got, the natural order of the universe meant that there was going to be another inhale breath. It was inevitable.

Applying the rhythm of breath to relationships

1. The inhale is how we receive love and allow it to infiltrate our cells and our love vibrations.
2. The pause at the top represents how we hold on to that love, sit in that love and bask in it.
3. The exhale is reflective of how we give love but also how we surrender to love rather than push it away or resist it.
4. The pause at the bottom is how we sit having given love before receiving it again (so tricky).

Now let's apply this to the energetic pattern of my romantic relationships. Here goes!

1. Receiving love is the best! Give me all the kisses, and you be the big spoon!
2. This is where I will pause at the top of the breath and bask in the yumminess of love. But there *will* be a point during that pause where I'm going to want to give that love back.
3. Inevitably, I exhale and reciprocate love. It feels good to give love. In fact, sometimes I love this more—it lights up parts of me that feel so, so good.

4. But when I'm pausing at the bottom of that breath, having given love and yet to receive more in return, how does that feel? Umm, scary and tricky! Do I keep giving love while getting nothing in return? Should I have to? I waver, I question my partner and myself during that pause at the bottom. But it's all about leaning into the cycle knowing that the inhale is inevitable.

I use the energetic qualities of the breath a lot in my business. Running your own business is terrifying 75 per cent of the time. The other 25 per cent of the time you're either celebrating a win, eating or sleeping. Some weeks there is an abundance of money coming in, tickets start selling like hot cakes, social media performs well and new clients are knocking down the door. Other weeks, all of the bills come in, taxes are due, tickets aren't selling, nobody seems to like your hilarious and well-thought-out social-media posts and clients are cancelling sessions one after another. There is so much that is unknown. There is so much that cannot be guaranteed. But never ever have I been thrown out on the street. Never ever have I been thrown in a jail cell for not paying my bills. Never ever have I lost all of my clients or failed to find new ones. I remind myself of these things whenever things look a little bleak, and if I'm patient, soon enough a new inhale sweeps through and things start moving again.

But here's the clincher: you have to allow this cycle time and space to happen. And this is where the balance between action and faith takes place. In those moments, knowing what you know about how the Law of Rhythm works, can you have faith and trust that everything will be okay? Can you be patient and wait for that inhale? Or will you flounder, freak out and try to fix, solve and do, do, do?

PRACTISING NON-ATTACHMENT AND 'THIS OR SOMETHING BETTER'

Non-attachment is the ability to detach oneself from a specific outcome. How is it even possible to not attach to something that you're trying to manifest? A manifestation comes out of a desire for something, so are we meant to just abandon that desire?

Again, we're only human, and when you want something badly, it's easy to become fixated on it. Especially when you're setting an intention, feeling into the vibrations around it and taking conscious action towards it, right? But this is where the faith part of the Manifestation Equation really gets its moment to shine.

You need to be able to have faith that if this intention is in your highest interest then it will absolutely manifest. If it doesn't, well that's because something better is on its way. We touched on this in Chapter 2, and I'm not gonna sugar-coat it; this can be hard to wrap your head around, especially when you're in a moment of extreme disappointment because things seemingly haven't played out how you expected. But if you're patient, and if you're willing to trust and observe, then I can guarantee (courtesy of a butt load of experience) that it's because there is something a zillion times better on its way.

When you attach to an intention, you place a certain level of expectation around it and automatically limit yourself by creating parameters and boundaries around the potential outcome. Your manifestation is no longer in your highest interest but in your perceived idea of what your highest interest is.

When I was twenty-one, I was offered the opportunity to nanny for an Australian family that was moving to London for 12 months. They wanted to fly me to the UK so I could live in their house in Chelsea, look after their kids four-and-a-half days a week and holiday with them in the south of France. At the time, the opportunity for me was golden. I had nothing really going on at home, I was single, working in a bakery and taking time off from studying, so I said yes. I quit my job, sublet my apartment, moved a bunch of stuff into storage and waited for that plane ticket to arrive in my inbox. Two days before I was scheduled to fly, the mother pulled the plug on the whole affair.

Here I was homeless, jobless and immensely disappointed. I had planned out the next year of my life in the UK, holidaying in Nice and living the Chelsea lifestyle. I couldn't believe my luck! All I could think about was what an amazing opportunity I'd just missed out on, not the fact that perhaps there was a reason it hadn't worked out.

The following week I fell in love (with Beau, who I've mentioned—you'll meet him officially later), moved back into my apartment with the girl (now my friend) who was subletting it from me, and I stayed in that apartment for 13 incredible years. I studied journalism and ended up having a pretty incredible eight-year career in food publishing. I often think about how different the trajectory of my life would have been had I hopped on that plane. I couldn't see it at the time, but I didn't go to London because there was something better on its way.

INTUITION

Psst, I want to let you in on a little insider information about faith and manifestation. I've addressed it several times in this chapter, but I really want you to grasp it fully before we proceed with the rest of this book. So here it is: at its deepest and most intimate level, manifestation is about learning to listen to your intuition in every moment. Once you can trust in your own internal knowing, you are able to act and create from a place of trust and divinity.

The faith you have in yourself is what ignites the rest of the Manifestation Equation. Once you're able to deeply trust your own thoughts, feelings and actions, then manifestation, and essentially creation, is just a natural by-product of that.

Intuition is the ability to know something instinctively without evidence, proof or conscious reasoning. It is a culmination of the senses, an awareness of vibrations, and it will often manifest as a 'gut instinct' or a 'feeling' about something or someone.

But often there is confusion about whether that internal voice (or feeling) is our intuition or the ego. In my experience, distinguishing between the two takes practice, but the biggest indicator and means of identification is the energy behind them.

The ego is often wearing a cloak made out of fear and insecurity. And while fear is designed to keep us safe, the ego uses fear as a means of protecting us from the unfamiliar. The energy of ego is from the outside in and can often feel restrictive and constrictive. The ego needs external validation in order to feel good, and its dialogue can be heard in the mind.

In contrast, intuition is dripping in truth and authenticity. It already believes you to be safe and operates from this space at all times. It acts from a place of abundance, and the energy of your intuition operates from the inside out. It wants you to experience joy and authentic expression. The voice of your intuition is felt rather than heard. It comes from the heart, feels expansive and uplifting, and doesn't require validation or justification.

We are not able to (nor should we) completely eradicate the ego. It does serve a purpose after all. The ego is our means of survival.

When it is functioning at a healthy level, its natural job is to protect us and keep us safe from dangerous things in the external world, like that blasted tiger in the jungle or an abusive relationship. Self-preservation says, 'I believe this to be unsafe' and therefore makes the self a priority. When the ego is over-inflated however, the self becomes priority over everything else, even when self-preservation isn't an issue. Symptoms of this are selfishness, self-indulgence, self-pity and, often, self-loathing.

In his book *Breaking the Habit of Being Yourself*, Dr Joe Dispenza describes the ego when it's under duress, and the ways in which an over-inflated ego can begin to warp our manifestations. He explains that the ego is often preoccupied with predicting the play-by-play and outcome of every situation and, based on this, the ego forms its own reality. And the problem with this is, as Dispenza points out, 'the more often we define reality through our sense, the more this reality becomes our law. Whatever we place our awareness on is our reality.'

So how do we begin to strengthen and give awareness to our intuition and pay less attention to our ego? If you're not sure who's steering the ship, ask yourself if your inner knowing is coming from a place of fear, and question it! Am I in danger? Am I at risk? Am I basing this decision on past experience? Am I making an assumption about the future? If you answer yes to any or all of these questions, try revisiting your relationship with fear.

In her book *Big Magic*, Elizabeth Gilbert speaks of fear's ability to hinder our creativity when we give it too much power. 'Basically, your fear is like a mall cop who thinks he's a Navy SEAL: He hasn't slept in days, he's all hopped up on Red Bull, and he's liable to shoot at his own shadow in an absurd effort to keep everyone "safe".'

Gilbert suggests not trying to abolish fear, but rather making some space for it. (Say what?!) By making space for fear to be comfortable, you are less likely to want to fight it, and it's less likely to want to fight you. I like this idea ...

Do you know what dampens fear? Many people say love, but I reckon it's faith. Fear comes from a future projection of the unknown. We fear what we can't see, predict, choose or guarantee. Faith is a deep knowing that you are capable, protected and on purpose, always.

We are all born as intuitive beings with the same intuitive abilities, but over time the ego muffles intuition's quiet and dulcet tones. Tuning back into your intuition just requires faith and a little practise. There is not a single soul on the planet that knows you better than you. So when a decision needs to be made, a step needs to be taken or a chapter needs to be closed, there is nobody better equipped to navigate the best way through than you.

I have read A LOT of self-help books trying to find the answers. Every time I get to the last page, I think I've figured it out as I adopt a new way of approaching an old situation. But while education is important and discovering new tools can be transformational, all of the answers I've ever needed were inside of me the whole time. Although that, too, sounds like classic self-help lingo, the answers actually are inside you ... like for real!

To be able to develop your intuition, faith in yourself is crucial. And the only way to trust in yourself, believe in yourself and listen to yourself is to *like* yourself. You wouldn't have a bar of someone you didn't respect, enjoy spending time with or you thought wasn't smart, deserving or worthy, would you? Well, unfortunately this is how many of us feel about ourselves! And until you strengthen your self-love, self-worth and self-trust, you'll struggle to strengthen your intuition and ultimately manifestation will escape you.

In Chapter 9 we'll tackle manifesting self-love and self-worth because I wholeheartedly believe, without a doubt, that in order to manifest any of the fun stuff like love, money and opportunity, you need to be able to think you're the best thing since gluten-free, sprouted thickly sliced bread.

There is a common misconception about intuition that I didn't discover until recently, and I'm not going to keep it to myself because it has completely transformed my ability to trust the voice of my intuition, always. So here it is: we often doubt our intuitive ability when we discover we were wrong about a person or situation that our gut was so god damn sure about. Numerous times I have been so sure that something was 'off' about someone or something only to be pleasantly surprised when that wasn't the case. On the flip side, I've also had a 'really good feeling' about some stuff and then been shocked by how off the mark I was. But here's the thing with your intuition, it guides you to exactly where you need to be.

What can appear to be you misreading a situation and not being able to trust your ability to make beneficial choices is actually your intuition leading you through a necessary experience.

Not so long ago, I met a guy. Let's not even bother giving him a name. I had such a good feeling about him. Intuitively, it felt wonderful. Vibrationally, we were aligned. Sparks were flying, conversations were in-depth, laughs they were aplenty. I stopped myself from being cautious (as had been my pattern in the past), and I allowed myself to fully open up and be vulnerable from the beginning (my intuition said it was safe to). Through the whole experience, my intuition led me to glorious places with this man, and then suddenly without warning he ended it. Now, more disappointing than the loss of a potential long-term lover was the fact that I had gotten it so wrong! How could my intuition have been so off?! My ego piped up and said, 'If I can't trust my own instincts, I'm f*cked!' My ego was bruised because I hadn't let it protect me, and consequently I had been rejected and found myself throwing an intimate pity party for one.

But when I really sat with this rejection, I realised that I had needed this experience. It enabled me to realise that rejection is something I can absolutely survive (relatively unscathed) and that avoiding experiences out of fear of rejection would not be something I'd have to worry about in the future, because it had already happened. My intuition led me there intentionally. This lesson was something I needed to learn, and if it hadn't been with him, it would have been with somebody else.

Can you think of a time where you believed your intuition had led you astray only to realise that, even though things hadn't worked out the way you'd planned, you were able to benefit from the experience in the long run? Keep this in mind the next time you question your intuition.

It works under the same guise as 'this, or something better'. Trusting that whatever is unfolding is for your benefit, and that your intuition is leading you there because both your higher self and the universe want what's best for you, ALWAYS.

Recognising your intuition

We can experience intuitive knowing in lots of different ways, and when people say they're not intuitive, or they don't know how to recognise their intuition, I've found it's usually because they're under the assumption that you can only identify it by one means. But this is not the case. Psychic sensitivity is often described using the term 'clair senses'. There are eight of these clair senses, and the four explored below are the ones that intuition most commonly and clearly communicates through. Many of us access our intuition through these senses, often without even realising it.

Clairvoyance: This is the sense of clear seeing. You may visualise situations, colours, people or signs that give you a clear picture of how to proceed.

Clairaudience: This is the sense of clear hearing. You know when people say, 'I heard a message?' That confused me for so long because I don't hear nuffin', but many people hear an audible cue when they're deep in meditation or reflection.

Clairsentience: This is the sense of clear feeling. You might feel people's vibrations and how they affect your own, it might manifest as butterflies, or just that 'gut feeling' I keep referring to.

Claircognisance: This is the sense of clear knowing. I believe we all possess this skill, we just choose to question and doubt ourselves constantly. Being able to trust your inner knowing is a superpower, and it will give you extra credit when it comes to manifesting.

You might use more than one of the clair senses; I use a combination of clairsentience and claircognisance. I get a feeling about a situation. Sometimes it manifests physically, like that time I went for a job interview and had to excuse myself to go the bathroom and vomit. They offered me the job, but I didn't take it because, spew! Sometimes it's just an overall feeling of joy or peace around a person or experience. My claircognisance is getting stronger the more I trust myself, but it takes practise and being okay with not always getting it 'right', knowing that however it works out is perfect for you in the moment.

SO, WHAT HAVE WE LEARNED?

★ Faith and religion are not one and the same.

★ Religion is based on a system of beliefs adopted from a set of teachings passed down through generations and ultimately taught or shared in the name of a higher power.

★ Faith is our drive to search for meaning, purpose and significance in life. It is based on our own personal belief systems and on having the confidence to trust so deeply in ourselves that we're able not just to believe, but also *to know* that there is a force much greater than ourselves always working in our favour.

★ Trust takes practise and requires you to treat each experience as separate and new.

★ Tapping into and following the Law of Rhythm helps us to understand all universal cycles and what they teach us about trust.

★ There is yin and yang energy within each universal cycle.

★ Practising non-attachment is one of the fundamental teachings of manifestation. It helps strengthen the faith that whatever happens is in your best interest.

★ Intuition and ego often get confused. Ego operates from a place of fear and insecurity, while intuition comes from a deep sense of safety and knowing.

★ The opposite of fear is faith.

★ The only way to strengthen your intuition is to work on your self-love, self-worth and self-trust. Without these things, manifestation will evade you.

★ There are several different ways you can access your intuition using the clair senses.

CHAPTER 7

A Few Manifestation Guidelines

I'm not about to throw a bunch of rules at you. No, no, no. That ain't my style at all. But now that you know the theory behind each individual part of the Manifestation Equation, I thought it might be helpful (and responsible of me) to share some 'best practice' tips with you.

Manifestation is no small task, and the things that you are going to make happen have the potential to be life-changing not just for you, but for everyone in your orbit. The ripple effect of conscious manifestation needs to be considered because, and excuse me while I go real big for a second, your manifestations could potentially change the world. But before we start talking global domination, let's go over some of the guidelines I abide by in my own manifestation practice. I'll explain what they are and why I think they're important, and you can decide to take them or leave them.

MINDFUL MANIFESTING

Often, when I speak of the power of our thoughts and feelings, and how we sometimes manifest things in our lives subconsciously (my shoulder dislocations, for example), it freaks people out because it leads them to believe they have little control over their potential manifestations. But I share these examples of how feelings and thoughts can manifest when we ignore them or when we give them too much airtime not to scare you, but because I want to illustrate how powerful you could be if you were manifesting things consciously.

Subconscious manifestation is the end game, but before we can learn to manifest wonderful things with our subconscious, we need to learn how to manifest with conscious intention. Once you get the hang of conscious manifestation, it will become an innate quality and a natural part of how you operate as a human.

Our subconscious is in charge of regulating basic physical bodily functions such as breathing, managing body temperature, and keeping our heart beating and our blood pumping, but it's also regulating our mind. Just as the body automatically filters carbon dioxide out of your system after you breathe in fresh oxygen, the subconscious filters out information that doesn't agree with what you already *believe* to be true. Instead, it presents thoughts, feelings and impulses that mirror the past (i.e. what you already know or have experienced).

I used to talk about my subconscious mind as if it was a separate entity, but the subconscious mind responds to what YOU have programmed it to do. Unfortunately, our programs have been running for so long we can't even remember how the data was originally entered. But by placing conscious intent around new ways of thinking, feeling and acting, we can begin to reprogram our subconscious. Conscious manifestation will begin that mind makeover by essentially taking the steering wheel and driving you to your ideal future.

It all starts with an intention. You consciously created the five intentions you've been working with in Part One of this book. Sure, you pulled some of them from your subconscious during the free-writing exercise, but you consciously turned those desires into your intentions by writing them down, attaching feelings to them, deciding on action steps you could take to get one step closer to each of them and believing that you are fully supported by the universe to receive those intentions as full-blown manifestations.

You can set conscious intentions whenever you like, but I like to have a date in the calendar each and every month that keeps me accountable. My favourite time to set intentions is the new moon, but for you it might be the first day of the month or the second Sunday in every month— whatever works. I find a month a good amount of time to give an intention an opportunity to unfold, perhaps not to its full bloom, but at least for your thoughts and feelings to find alignment and your first few action steps to create forward momentum.

In Chapter 3, I outlined some basic intention-setting tips. If you've got some time up your sleeve (it's for the betterment of your life, I promise), I'd like to expand on some of those points just a little.

Forget about the details

The who, what, why, when and how of an intention can be so hard to let go of, especially when you're hell-bent on a specific outcome. But now that you've learned about non-attachment and are able to trust in 'this, or something better', you can see the importance of not fixating on specifics. All these details do is fence you in to a set of parameters built by your own subconscious.

I love the way Dr Joe Dispenza describes how manifestation should take us by surprise:

> *We should never be able to predict how our new creations will manifest; they must catch us off guard.*

When I was trying to manifest a book deal with a publisher so I could write this very book that you're reading, I was way too specific with my original intention, and it just wasn't happening for me. My original intention named a specific publisher (not the one I'm so grateful I ended up with), exactly how the deal would be offered to me, a publishing date (which was years off the original publishing date of this book) and the title of the book (which was very different to *Make It Happen*).

For a good six months I stuck rigidly to my intention as it was, and I felt the book deal slipping further and further away. So I stripped it right back and asked myself to identify the relevance and importance of this intention. When I landed said book deal, how did I want to feel? I figured out that all that was important to me was that my message was heard. It wasn't important that it be in book form (but yay that it is!). It certainly didn't need to be with the specific publisher I had in mind (and glory be that it wasn't), and the title and publishing date were irrelevant.

So my intention became: *My message around manifestation is heard and received by many. I feel on purpose, accomplished and full of excitement.*

BAM!

I had a meeting with my now-publisher within the month and signed a book deal the following month.

We humans are funny! We think we can control our future by re-creating a past experience, but creating an unknown reality requires a little bit of faith that the almighty all-knowing universe has bigger, bolder plans for us. Because often, we can only see with our eyes what our imagination can conjure up. If we can't conceive it then it can be very hard for us to see an opportunity, even if it's staring us in the face.

Mind your own (manifesting) business

Want a specific individual to fall in love with you? Want that person to change their mind or leave their relationship? Want someone you care about to start eating better? Want that 'guest' to finally move out of your house?

Well, the short answer is that you can't manifest for other people! (I know! It sucks!)

But just trust me on this one; I have tried several times. Not only does it not work, but it's also not okay ... whether you're doing it 'for other people', 'to change other people for the better' or 'to help people', it doesn't matter. However you twist the words, manifesting for other people is a big no-no for two main reasons:

1. **Logistically, it's a near impossible feat.** You cannot alter someone else's thoughts or feelings. You also can't make them take action or control their level of faith. So, according to the Manifestation Equation, you can see how it's near impossible to manifest for another person.

2. **Morally, it's not okay.** Essentially what you're implying when you attempt to manifest for someone else is that you want to mess around with his or her free will. Remember, they have their own destiny and future, which is being cared for by the universe. You don't get to meddle with that, especially without their consent.

What about if a loved one is unwell? Can't you manifest healing vibrations for them? NO! That still counts as manifesting for other people. (Don't shoot the messenger!) What you can do is set a vibrational standard around them. Focus on their healing rather than their illness, shower them with feelings of joy, happiness and love, and be an example of healthy action and good faith. By all means hold them in your thoughts and prayers, and dedicate your meditation or yoga practice to them, if that feels good, but do it out of compassion and not to alter their destiny or life path.

Practise gratitude

When you first start manifesting, it is very easy and very common to become so consumed with creating your future through your manifestations that you lose perspective on, and sometimes even appreciation for, what you already have in your life.

Trying to manifest a brand-new all-wheel drive to take the kids camping? Great, but are you expressing gratitude for the car you already have and the beautiful kids that you get to strap into it?

Practising gratitude for what you already have sends a very clear sign to the universe not only that you are ready to receive your future manifestations, but also that you'll appreciate them when they show up. I mean there's nothing like gifting someone a birthday present and not receiving a thank you. Am I right? (I know who's not getting a present next year.)

Research has shown that expressing gratitude improves our relationships, sleep, self-esteem, mental health and overall physical wellbeing. It's easy to see why it's one of the highest vibrations there is.

As you start successfully manifesting, it's also important to show gratitude and appreciation for the delivery of your intentions—even before they manifest. Remember when we were setting intentions and I asked you to write them in the present tense, as if you already had them? And then I asked you what it would feel like in your body if you had manifested your intentions? Same thing! Can you be grateful for your future manifestations, right now? Before they've come to life? Can you feel into the gratitude you'll be experiencing for them soon enough?

A typical gratitude list will outline the things we're already grateful for, such as our family, friends or job. The reason we're grateful for these things is because we're currently experiencing them, or we have previously experienced them. But what is preventing you from experiencing gratitude for the things you're yet to receive? Can you give thanks for what you're certain (because you have faith) will manifest in the not-too-distant future?

My mate Dr Joe Dispenza asks a similar question:

> Can you give thanks for something that exists as a potential, but has not yet happened in your reality? If so, you are moving from cause and effect (waiting for something outside of you to make a change inside of you) to causing an effect (changing something inside of you to produce an effect outside of you).

Once I introduced the small and effortless practice of gratitude to my manifestations, I started to notice a profound effect.

Don't just stand there, manifest!

Many of us get caught up in the mentality that we'll get to work making things happen when we have it all figured out. This keeps us so stuck. A common thing I hear ALL the time from my clients is this: 'When I have my finances/health/home sorted THEN I'll start manifesting love.'

Here's another classic, and one I was a slave to for years: 'When I lose five/ten/fifteen kilos, THEN I'll manifest that job/man/happiness.'

The universe will only give you what you are ready for, and I guarantee that you were born ready for most things, so your readiness has zero to do with the number on the bathroom scales. The weight-loss thing comes down to self-love and self-worth, and I've mentioned this a few times now, but until you improve the way you feel about yourself, you're right, you probably won't manifest your soulmate. And not because they won't love you five kilos heavier, but because YOU don't love you now, and you probs still won't when you're five kilos lighter.

I told myself countless times that I would become an author when I had become a contributor for X amount of websites, sold X amount of courses, had run X amount of events and, yes, when I had lost X amount of weight—as if there were some sort of official checklist that I had to tick off before I was worthy of writing a book. But then I realised that when I had reached the ever-shifting X, the goalposts would move, and the book would get further and further out of my reach.

If you're eternally striving for a feeling of completion and putting off your dreams until you 'arrive' at a specific destination, you're never gonna get there. So if you find yourself making excuses when you sit down to consciously set your intentions, put them to the side and set those intentions anyway because (newsflash!) none of us have it all figured out, and we probably never will. And that's okay. That should never prevent you from striving for bigger, bolder and brighter dreams.

We good?

Get real familiar with dharma and karma

Dharma and karma are two concepts that deserve more than a few paragraphs in one chapter of this book. But for the purposes of determining their role in the practice of manifestation, I will do my best to make sense of them succinctly.

Dharma is a broad concept from Buddhist and Hindu teachings, and it has many definitions but, at its essence, it is that which supports and sustains the universe. Following your own personal dharma is to be living with purpose and expressing yourself authentically. It is believed that this is the most impactful role you can play to be of service to the universe.

So, in the context of manifestation, dharma encourages you to manifest that which is on purpose and meaningful to your greater calling in this life. In doing so, collectively we are able to sustain and support the consciousness of the universe.

Karma differs from dharma in that it relates specifically to our actions, and it is best described by the universal law known as the Law of Cause and Effect, which states that **for every action there is an equal and opposite reaction**. But in simpler terms, and for the purposes of understanding karma's impact on manifestation, I believe that the universal Law of Cause and Effect can be described this way: for every thought, feeling and action there is a vibrational shift of energy, and with that shift in energy manifestation begins to occur. So be the vibrations you wish to see in the world, and give out what you desire to receive. Want more love? Be more loving. Want more money? Be generous with what you have.

The other side of karma is the karma you're already experiencing from past actions. And if you are indeed living out your karma, do you have a choice in what you are able to manifest? Later in the book you'll learn about soul contracts, which I believe is relevant to this discussion, but also know that we are never dealt a situation that we are not ready for. Lessons that we need to learn will manifest as they should, and we always have a choice in how we respond to them.

Let's get visual

If you're the kind of person who has to see something in order to believe it, I cannot recommend visualisation enough when it comes to your manifestation practice. At the conclusion of every Lunar Nights event, I take attendees through a powerful guided visualisation meditation. During this meditation, I ask them to visualise themselves already having manifested all of their desires. I encourage you to do the same, either by downloading my guided visualisation meditation (see page 337 for a link to this) or by doing the exercise opposite.

When I was first starting out with my manifestation practice, I would do this exercise every morning when I first woke up. There was something about those wee early-morning hours that made my ability to visualise stronger. Through my many manifestation experiments, I've also found that vibrations are easier to access and that they gain strength when combined with visualisation. Again, it's the sense of really being able to believe something that you can see playing out in front of you.

Exercise 8
SEE THE LIFE YOU WANT

Close your eyes and picture your life as it will be when you
have everything you desire to manifest.

What does a day in your life look like?

How does your day unfold?

Who is there?

What do you eat?

How do you play?

How does it feel to witness yourself in these states?

Feel free to get detailed with your visualisations. The more
clearly you can see these things, the more you will believe
they are possible.

PART TWO

THE
PRACTICE

CHAPTER 8

Manifesting the Little Things

As with most new endeavours, there are two principles that work every time: baby steps and practise. Both of these principles apply when it comes to the Manifestation Equation.

The most glorious thing about energy, vibrations and manifestation is that the universe doesn't value any one thing more than the other. So whether you're trying to manifest a car space or a brand new car, the universe values them equally.

And here's the thing: manifesting little things like car spaces, chance encounters, free coffees and books you've been meaning to read is bloody easy because you're not overly attached to the outcome. Without even being conscious of it, you're practising non-attachment!

My friends know me as the 'Manifesting Queen'. Not because of the large sums of money, the dream clients or the new car I've manifested, but because of the little everyday things I now manifest with such ease that I don't even have to do it consciously anymore.

As we progress through this chapter, you'll see that, when it comes to manifesting the little things, some parts of the equation hold less weight than others. But as we progress through the rest of the book and start manifesting bigger things, you'll notice that each part of the equation plays just as integral a role as the next. (Just something to be aware of.)

No matter what it is you want to consciously manifest, big or small, start by looking at how you can apply each part of the Manifestation Equation and go from there. I've seen even the most sceptical would-be manifesters surprise themselves, so come on. What do you have to lose?

Step 1 THOUGHTS

What is my intention?

Step 2 FEELINGS

How will I feel when that intention manifests?

Step 3 ACTIONS

What action can I take towards making
it happen?

Step 4 FAITH

Have faith that it will manifest in a way that will
best serve you and your highest interest.

LET'S START SMALL

Here are some things you might like to try manifesting before attempting
some of the bigger undertakings.

PARKING SPACES

I live in a busy beachside suburb, perhaps the busiest beachside suburb in
Sydney. On the weekends, residents of my neighbourhood don't move
their cars out of fear that they won't be able to park anywhere closer
than half an hour's walk away from their house. I just don't want to live
my life like that, so when I first started playing around with manifestation
I would use my skills to manifest not just a free parking space, but one
right outside my front door. This worked for me time and time again, and
it was all down to using the Manifestation Equation.

If a space wasn't there when I arrived, it wouldn't be a big deal. I'd just drive around until I found one. And because I wasn't emotionally invested in the outcome, it didn't become a limiting belief or negative story that I carried with me if one didn't show up. I'd just try again next time.

Now you give it a go.

Exercise 9
FIND THAT SWEET SPOT

Step 1: Set an intention as you approach the area you want to park in. 'I have a rock-star car park right out the front of my apartment building/in the shopping centre/at the beach.' Visualise an empty space, ready to drive into.

Step 2: Tap into the feeling of having that car space. It might be excitement, relief or success. Hold on to that feeling as you visualise yourself approaching the parking space.

Step 3: See yourself simply driving into the car space. Easy!

Step 4: Have complete faith the whole way home that a car space will be waiting for you when you arrive. No time for freaking out about having to drive around for 30 minutes, no feelings of frustration directed at tourists for parking inconsiderately, and no worries because you are certain that car spot is waiting for you to drive into.

BOOKS

There's a community book exchange at the end of my street. It's a beautiful example of energy exchange in that you donate a book and take a book to read. Quite often, when people are doing a clear out, they will dump several books at a time, so there are new books popping up almost daily. I like to use this book exchange to practise manifestation. You don't need a book exchange in your street to manifest a good read. Someone could lend you a book, gift you a book or leave one on the seat of the next bus you hop on. Remember not to get caught up in specifics. Just keep your eyes on the literary prize. Your turn.

Exercise 10
YOUR NEXT READ

Step 1: Decide which book you want to read, then visualise it on the shelf of the book exchange/library/café/your friend's house.

Step 2: Tap into the feeling of having that book in your hands. How good does that feel?

Step 3: Actively keep your eyes peeled every day when you are out and about, and await its arrival. You are going about your business, and you're not attached to the outcome.

Step 4: Hold the firm belief that it will turn up, because it will.

HOUSEMATES

This category is definitely higher stakes than a parking spot or a book (there are few things riskier than a dodgy housemate, amirite?), but it's a good one to experiment with because the stakes aren't as high as they are if you're manifesting the love of your life or that dream career. So let's consider this one a warm-up to those biggies.

I've had to manifest a new housemate several times, and having many housemates has taught me what I do and don't want in a living companion. So I became super clear about what I did want. This is where all manifestations should start, regardless of what it is you're trying to manifest. How do you want to feel? For me, my home environment needs to feel comfortable, inviting, drama-free and supportive. Once I have that sorted, I'm good to go. If you share your living space with other people, this next exercise might be a good one for you to try.

Exercise 11
FIND THE PERFECT FLATTIE!

Step 1: Set your intention: 'I live with the perfect housemate. Our house is harmonious, inviting and supportive.'

Step 2: Tap into the feelings you want to experience in your home as often as possible. Create a vibration around them so your house also starts vibrating on the frequency that you're looking to attract.

Step 3: The next step is to take action to find a housemate. #obviously! Ask friends, post an ad on your social media and be active in your approach.

Step 4: Finally, have faith that the perfect housemate for you will turn up. I mean, why would the universe deliver anything less than that, right?

If it all sounds too simple, it's because it is. And the more you practise with the simple stuff, the better. Also, remember not to entertain thoughts of not finding the right housemate or making the wrong choice, as these thoughts serve no purpose. By envisaging the worst-case scenario, you'll just invite it into your house. #beentheredonethat

SMALL AMOUNTS OF MONEY

We'll get around to manifesting the big bucks in a later chapter, but let's start small and build up your confidence. How about we start with five dollars?

Exercise 12
BET YOU FIVE BUCKS
YOU CAN MANIFEST THIS ONE!

Step 1: Set the intention. 'I have five extra dollars in my wallet.'

Step 2: How would manifesting five dollars make you feel?

Step 3: What action steps could you take? (This is actually an interesting one, because by not spending five dollars on something you ordinarily would, like a second coffee, you are in fact gaining five dollars, but I digress.)

Step 4: Believe that it is absolutely possible that you can manifest this money.

Make sure you keep your eyes open for this one. You might find this money on the street (but not likely). It will most likely manifest as a voucher, a discount on a regular purchase, a refund, a free coffee or even a note in the pocket of your jeans. Remember to abandon your perceived idea of how it will arrive and just keep your eyes open to all the possibilities.

Okay, let's take things up a notch

Now that you've had a little practise, let's up the stakes a little. Here are examples of other little things that can be manifested. Some of these are a little outside the box, so stay with me.

WEARING AN INVISIBILITY CLOAK

I've made it very clear that you can't manifest for other people or make someone do anything against his/her own free will. You can, however, control your own energetic vibration, and that means protecting yourself from people that you don't wish to see. Let me put this in context.

After a very complicated relationship with an ex-boyfriend (more on him later), I decided it would be best for both of us if we didn't see each other for a while. There were a few problems with this plan, though: not only did we live in the same suburb, but we also lived a mere two streets away from each other, shared a bunch of mutual friends and had such a strong connection that we always seemed to end up in the same locations, no matter how random or obscure. But I needed space. We both did.

So I decided to take a leaf out of Harry Potter's spellbook and place an invisibility cloak over both of us. I set an intention that even if we were in the same place, I would not see him and he would not see me. And for two whole years this worked a treat. We inhabited the same neighbourhood and never, not once, did we catch so much as a side-glance of each other. How did I do it? Well, I'm no Hermione, just a wizard of manifestation! Is there someone you could use a breather from? It's worth a try.

After two years had passed and I decided I was ready to come out of 'hiding', my ex and I were texting and he asked me how we'd never run into each other even though we lived so close to each other. I thought about telling him, but instead responded with the shrugging shoulders emoji. I mean, a girl can't reveal all of her secrets.

Exercise 13
THE INVISIBILITY CLOAK

Step 1: Begin with the intention: 'X and I will not cross paths. I am invisible to them and they are invisible to me.'

Step 2: Tap into the importance of this and how it will make you feel: relaxed, calm, safe and free.

Step 3: Take the necessary action steps to facilitate this. For example, do your best not to tempt fate by walking past their house or dropping by their favourite spots. But equally, don't go out of your way to avoid places you may see them because the whole point is to not live in fear.

Step 4: Believe without a doubt that you will not run into each other and that the universe will support this in any way possible.

SOMETHING YOU REALLY WANT, BUT DON'T NECESSARILY WANT TO BUY

Let's be realistic here, I'm not talking about manifesting a Tesla (though that would be cool), I'm thinking more along the lines of a bunch of flowers or a winter coat. One time I manifested five kilos of protein powder. To be honest, I didn't manifest this with conscious intent, but I can see how it happened when I look back on the circumstances. I was working as a recipe developer at the time, so I always had a pantry of random ingredients left over from various projects. I had made my way through various samples of protein powder after using it in my morning smoothies, so I thought I should probably just go and buy some more. But you know these powders can be expensive, and I wasn't sure exactly what variety I wanted. I decided not to overthink it and trusted that there would just be more protein powder when I needed it. Within days, I was offered a project developing recipes for a new brand of hemp protein powder, and on the same day I took the job they couriered five kilos of the stuff directly to my front door.

How did this happen? Let's run through the steps!

Step 1: I had the thought that I needed protein powder.

Step 2: There was feeling behind this thought because I wanted the protein powder for my smoothies and it mattered to me that I get some. But at the same time I wasn't attached to the idea.

Step 3: I took action by researching different powders and asking people which ones they would recommend.

Step 4: I guess I just trusted that I would get protein powder one way or another … and what do you know, I did!

I find this such a funny example of what can happen when you start getting the hang of manifestation; things that you want (even super-random ingredients from your pantry!) will just start appearing, seemingly out of nowhere.

RECEIVE THE SIGNS THE UNIVERSE IS SENDING YOU

This one is more about allowing a channel of communication between you and the universe than it is about following the Manifestation Equation. Sometimes, in order to have complete faith that you're being supported, it's nice to receive a little sign or some sort of confirmation that the universe is paying attention. The first thing to do is decide what that sign will be. It might be a feather, a butterfly, a number or a song. It could be anything really, just as long as it's something you don't stumble across all the time. For example, choosing a leaf as your sign of choice is probably not a great indicator, since there are leaves on just about every inch of pavement.

The song 'Harvest Moon' by Neil Young is one of my signs that the universe has my back, and whenever I need some confirmation, it always seems to play. I recall getting ready to go out on a date with this guy that I REALLY liked. I was having a little bit of a freak out, and in a conversation with the universe before said date I asked for a sign that everything was going to be okay. I hopped in my Uber, and 'Harvest Moon' was playing on the radio. I arrived at the bar where I was meeting him, and 'Harvest Moon' started playing the minute I sat down. I thanked the universe (because gratitude is important), and I instantly felt at ease knowing I was being fully supported.

If only manifesting financial abundance and your soulmate were as easy as manifesting the little things, hey? Well, according to the universe, it is! Remember, as far as the universe is concerned, little things and big things are equal; we are the ones giving those 'big' things more weight than we should. So, with that in mind, let's move on to manifesting the big stuff.

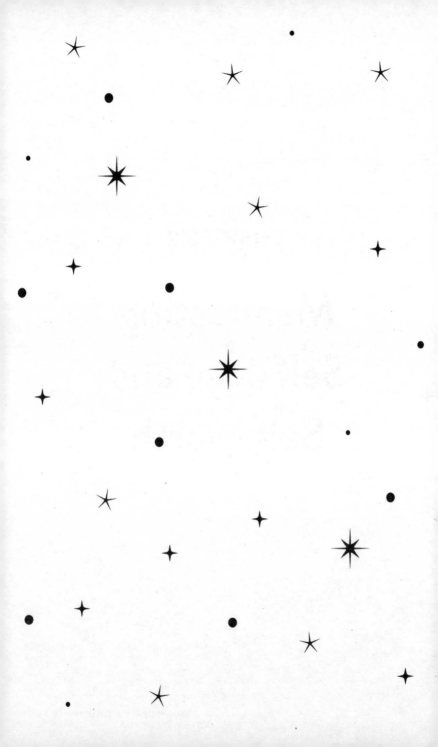

CHAPTER 9

Manifesting Self-love and Self-worth

When I was thirteen, my breast started grow. Yep, just the one—the right one to be specific. My left breast was still clutching onto pre-pubescence for dear life. But that right one, well she had a mind of her own. At first it was no big deal, just a little bit of asymmetry. 'It's completely normal,' my mother would say. 'Most women have breasts that vary in size.' (Hers didn't. They were perfect, perky C-cups.) But when the difference between them approached more than a standard cup size, we went to see the doctor. 'Oh yes, completely normal,' the middle-aged male GP professed. 'Nothing to worry about. That left one will catch up in no time at all.'

But by the age of fifteen, my right breast was a D-cup and my left breast was only an A-cup. By this point, my mother had taken me to countless specialists including (but not limited to) a paediatrician, endocrinologist, paediatric endocrinologist, naturopath, traditional Chinese medicine practitioner, herbalist, kinesiologist, Ayurvedic doctor, acupuncturist and ... well, to be honest, they all blurred into one big disappointment. Each gave me a variation of 'We can't find a definitive reason for this, but I'm sure over time the left one will catch up.'

THE (B)ODYSSEY BEGINS

It didn't catch up. The size difference between my breasts was mortifyingly obvious, and it wasn't something I could hide under a baggy T-shirt. While all of my friends were enjoying their fifteen-year-old bodies, spending long days in their bikinis down at the beach, discovering their new curves and the interest of boys, I was rearranging a silicone bra insert (or 'chicken fillet', as I referred to it) into my D-cup bra and making excuses for why I couldn't swim that day (or do any other activity that risked said chicken fillet falling out).

I shut down. I didn't know how else to handle the complete lack of control I had over my body. While my friends were talking about making it to second base, I was avoiding second base at all costs—even avoiding accidental elbow grazes while in line at the canteen. I hid it well, but it felt like a gigantic secret that other girls my age couldn't handle, and before I knew it that secret became the division between my 'normal' teenage life and the real me.

The rest of my body was not immune to whatever (untraceable) hormonal dysfunction was taking place in my body. Although I led a very normal and healthy (for a teenager) life, my hips and thighs grew almost overnight. In what felt like a very cruel joke being played by the teenage body gods, I was also gifted vibrant purple stretch marks (due to the unexpected inflation of my curves) and a generous serving of cellulite.

None of my teenage friends had cellulite. Not one! I felt like the odd one out on so many fronts, and it was safe to say that by the age of fifteen I had grown to despise my very existence. My mother felt helpless. She did everything in her power to heal my relationship with my body. After exhausting all other avenues, she took me to see a cosmetic surgeon.

'I can't operate until her breasts stop growing,' the male surgeon explained. 'What if I put an implant in the left side and then it decides to grow? We'll be in a bit of a pickle then, won't we?' (I'm sure he didn't really speak like a character from a bedtime storybook, but his condescending tone meant he might as well have.) I begged and cried and sobbed and tantrummed and then sat silent. Mum stepped in and pleaded, 'They haven't budged in over a year. Please help her!'

Not one, not two, but three boob jobs later ...

Three months before my sixteenth birthday, they operated. I was technically still a child, so I spent my post-op recovery in the children's hospital. My friends came to visit, and I'm still not sure what they thought was wrong with me. I'd woven such a web of cover-ups and white lies by then, but I'm certain they didn't think they were visiting a friend who'd gone under the knife for half a boob job.

Ordinarily this surgery would have been the happy ending I'd been hoping for, but truthfully it was the beginning of a nightmare. Twelve days after surgery, I came down with a horrendous fever. The incision where they'd inserted the implant was weeping, and Mum was pretty certain it shouldn't be so hot, inflamed or yellow. That night I was diagnosed with a severe golden staph infection, and I spent the next ten days in hospital on an antibiotic drip. My surgeon suggested we remove the implant for a few months until the wound was healed, and then we'd try again.

'NOT AN OPTION!' I proclaimed. So as soon as I was taken off of the antibiotic drip, I was admitted to surgery, the implant was removed, the wound was cleaned out (then doused in industrial disinfectant) and the implant was popped back in.

Again, the wound did not heal. There was no infection this time; my body was simply rejecting this foreign object. I was admitted back into hospital, now sixteen and technically an adult, which meant I was no longer welcome in the children's ward. I recovered post surgery (my third recovery in two months) in a hospital surrounded by adults. It seemed fitting. In the past six months, I had aged beyond my teenage years. In fact, I felt like I had missed them completely.

The final surgery was a success (thank goodness, because it was likely to be the last attempt). Although I now had two almost-D-cup breasts (one slightly perkier and firmer than the other), I was so traumatised by the experiences of achieving this that my ghastly low self-esteem barely got a bump. To top things off, I'd been pumped with three general anaesthetics in the space of three months, six courses of antibiotics, on top of the ten-day intravenous antibiotic drip, several high doses of morphine post surgeries, and god knows how many packets of strong painkillers.

Perhaps unsurprisingly, this part of my life is a bit of a blur. I had to call Mum and ask about a lot of these details because, to be frank, I've blocked a lot of them out.

But what followed was just as harrowing ...

A 'normal' body, but at what cost?

Feeling betrayed by my own body, lying to all of my friends and trying desperately to recover from some pretty intense narcotics for a sixteen-year-old, I was wrapping up my second-to-last year of high school and beginning my HSC. I had always excelled at school, but suddenly I found it really hard. The months in hospital had definitely put me behind, but this was bigger than that—the information wasn't penetrating. I lost all motivation and became disinterested in my friends. I cried a lot. I was depressed, distressed and then one afternoon I skipped the final few periods of school and took a packet of sedatives to the local cliffs to quieten the voices in my head.

I got through ten pills by the time the police and my dad found me huddled in a cliff cave. I wasn't trying to kill myself. I'm actually not sure what I was trying to do. Perhaps it was a cry for help. I was admitted back to the hospital (my home away from home) and force-fed charcoal until I vomited up the entire contents of my stomach. I was sent home with a referral for a psychiatrist.

The psychiatrist diagnosed me with post-traumatic stress, and it was suggested that I be homeschooled until my mental health 'improved'. Although I had exemptions and leniency for the HSC, I still failed. Failed! Me! I was NOT a student who failed their HSC. I was a smart kid with loads of potential (hey, I had the report cards to prove it).

So now I not only had a body I couldn't control, but I'd also lost my smarts and I'd pretty much wasted my dad's hard-earned money on a failed private-school education. #disappointment (At least that's the way I saw it at the time.)

When I left school, I got my shit together by putting bandaids over everything. I had a sweet and cruisy boyfriend who was a wonderful first love—he didn't even notice the perkier left breast! I managed to go and study journalism despite that tragic final year at school, and I got my mental health sorted thanks to a curiosity in meditation, self-help and that gorgeous yoga teacher, Dan (you remember him).

Sounds impressive, right? But like I said, these things were all bandaids. I hadn't dealt with any of the deeper issues that plagued me. As far as I was concerned, my body had still failed me. Not one professional, not even the top paediatric endocrinologist in Australia at the time, had been able to tell me why that left breast never grew. A generic, 'Sometimes this kind of thing just happens' wasn't good enough for me, and with no explanation to turn to, I subconsciously berated and punished my body for letting me down.

A side effect, I believe, of all of the drugs, anaesthetics, stress and trauma I had experienced in my mid-teens, coupled with the mysterious cause of the asymmetry in my body, resulted in a serious struggle with my weight in my twenties.

The final straw

No matter how little I ate or how much I exercised, I could not shift weight. I held it all in my butt and my thighs, and even though I did everything you were 'meant' to do (plus extra), it just wouldn't budge. I ate exceptionally well, drank heaps of water and minimal alcohol, did yoga, ate superfoods, drank green juices, and exercised (often three times a day), but I just couldn't get where I wanted to go. It wasn't long before an exercise addiction masquerading as a love for exercise escalated into complete adrenal burn out, rendering me unable to do any type of exercise without collapsing in a heap.

I had every test from every traditional, holistic and alternative health professional in the city. Every time I turned up to an appointment, tried a new supplement, attempted a new treatment or read a new study, I thought 'this is it! This is the answer.' But it never was. Again, my body was failing me.

I grew up by the beach, but I dreaded every summer. Not only because I was ashamed of my body, but also because I didn't want people to think I didn't care for my body. I did all of the same things that my slim, fit and bikini-body gorgeous friends did, and I did varying amounts of exercise depending on my adrenal status. But I was puffy, cellulite-ridden and, dare I say it, fat.

So when the self-love/body love wave came crashing through popular culture in about 2010, in what seemed like a buzzword tsunami, I just couldn't get on board with it. How could I love my body when it wasn't listening to me or responding to me? And if I couldn't love my body, I was convinced that others couldn't love it either. Being naked in front of people was my worst nightmare, and this made dating an anxiety-ridden experience. As women often do, I catastrophised the event of undressing long before the first kiss. I predicted shock, horror, violent rejection, laughter and disappointment, and I'd convince myself that these men deserved better.

In my thirty-five years, eight men have seen me naked (sorry, Dad!) and not one of them has reacted any other way than wanting to jump my bones (again, so sorry, Dad!). All of them praised my curves, none of them were concerned about the slight asymmetry of my breasts, and there most certainly has never been any pointing, laughing or blatant rejection ... until recently, but we'll get to that in a minute.

Whenever I felt down about my body, I knew I could always fall back on my quick wit, intelligence and sparkling personality, but when I started working for Annabel, I momentarily lost all of those things, too.

I'd picked myself up after that dismal final year of high school and made pretty good use of my smarts by climbing corporate ladders and being rewarded for my intelligence in the workplace. But for the first time since high school, I started to slide backwards. Annabel let me know, in various ways, that I wasn't clever enough, smart enough, fast enough, meticulous enough or good enough. I mean, she could have dropped all the adjectives and just said I wasn't enough.

At first, I wasn't buying it; I knew I was enough of all of those things. But after working sixty-hour weeks and facing her negativity day in and day out for a year, I started to believe her. I was exhausted, riddled with stress, overweight, battling brain fog and had burned out my adrenals as well as many friendships and my relationship. You know what? By the end of that year, I probably *wasn't* enough. I felt like nothing.

This was my rock bottom. This was me days away from checking myself into a psych ward.

That was five years ago ...

FAST-FORWARD TO THE PRESENT-DAY JORDANNA

A couple of months ago, I met a man. He was wonderful, and the first man I'd felt any connection with in almost two years. Sparks were flying, we had similar interests, the same values, our conversations were deep, our laughs were genuine and our spirits were kindred. He was also a very honest and kind man (something I hadn't had the pleasure of experiencing in a very long time). It was beyond refreshing, and I'd be lying if I said I wasn't a little bit excited about the potential of this relationship.

We got three dates deep with no kiss. For all his positive attributes, his one flaw (although I actually found it incredibly endearing) was that he was a little 'awkward' at times, so I put this 'no kiss' thing down to nervousness. After all, it does get increasingly harder to go in for a pash once you've grown out of the binge-drinking, house-party phase of life.

But alas, the no-kiss thing was *not* due to his inability to make a move: 'I feel a deep emotional, mental and spiritual connection with you,' he said, 'and I love our conversations and I love spending time with you, but ...' (uh oh, buts are never good) 'I'm just not physically attracted to you.'

Breathe, Jord. Just breathe.

When one of your greatest fears materialises in real life, it's RARELY as monumental as your mind would have you believe it will be. To have a man look you square in the eyes and tell you he is not physically attracted to you even though he's attracted to you on every other level is definitely something every girl should experience at least once (hopefully only once!). Of course it stings, but how you feel after hearing something like this is a true indicator of where the needle on your self-love and self-worth barometer is sitting.

I thanked him for his honesty, declined his invitation to 'just be friends' (umm I've learned that lesson before) and went to meet a girlfriend for a wine and a giggle.

Jord five years earlier would not have survived that universal test. She would have crumpled, not eaten for an entire week, punished herself at the gym and probably googled nose jobs, liposuction and 'how to cut bangs at home'.

But thankfully I had spent the last few years making self-love and my own self-worth a top priority. When I started learning more about manifestation, it became clearer to me that loving yourself was paramount in order to be the curator and creator of your own life. If you want to be able to stand in your truth and show up as the most authentic version of you, you need to be able to love and be goddamn proud of your own authenticity, otherwise what's the bloody point?

When that man rejected me (with all of my clothes on) and I was able to say 'I appreciate your honesty' and walk away, and then laugh about it with my friend, I knew I'd upgraded, and you can, too.

ALL FACETS OF MANIFESTATION BEGIN WITH A HIGH VIBRATION OF SELF

It is imperative that you feel worthy of your manifestations in order for them to materialise. There is absolutely no way of getting around this. A high level of self-worth and the ability to unequivocally love yourself will impact your ability to manifest money, love, career, happiness, everything! Without it you'll struggle. The answers you're seeking can't be found externally, in the same way the many, many health professionals I visited about my chest and weight problems weren't able to help me heal from roughly twenty years of telling my body it was disgusting, unworthy, disappointing and a failure.

If I can go from Lopsided Lucy, a high-school failure and a punching bag for a narcissistic boss, to the girl who shrugs off flat-out rejection by a potential suitor based solely on her physical appearance, then you can start to believe in the brilliance that is you.

But it's going to take some conscious work. You'll be squeezing the most from each of the four parts of the Manifestation Equation, and I encourage you to complete all of the exercises outlined in this chapter, no matter how uncomfortable they make you feel.

I spoke of spiritual sidestepping in Part One, and if you were to just skip or even skim this chapter, you would be doing just that—sidestepping. Just reading the words is not enough. You need to get in there and DO THE WORK. But it will be worth it. #promise

Self-love is not selfish or conditional

In Chapter 4, I used the analogy of filling up champagne glasses at a party to illustrate how, if your primary focus is getting everyone else tipsy, there won't be enough fancy French champagne left for you. This was in reference to the containment of your feelings, but the same principle applies to your self-love barometer.

Loving, giving, providing, nurturing, healing, fixing and creating for everyone else is wonderful and rewarding, but it's NEVER more important than doing all of those things for yourself first. Not *instead of* doing them for other people, just doing them for yourself *before* you do them for other people.

You are the priority. And when you make yourself the priority, it becomes a thousand times easier to be all of those things for the other people in your life. But somewhere along the line, 'self-love' seems to have become confused with body brushing, oil massage, green juices and meditation. While those things are lovely and you should absolutely do them if they make you feel good, that's not the kind of self-love I'm referring to.

You don't need to hit certain marks, pass certain tests or participate in certain practices in order to love yourself. We have strict criteria regarding when we are allowed to love ourselves: when my boobs are perfect; when my butt is smaller; when they say they love me; when I get that job; when I save that amount of money; when I feel happiness; when I lose the weight THEN I can love myself. But that love is conditional. If none of these things ever eventuate, are you not entitled to be loved?

Of course you are!

I fell victim to all of these conditions, especially the 'when I lose weight' one. I think many of us do. So how do we get past it? I started with something simple, by telling myself, 'I am not my weight.' And it's true; I'm not. Once I stopped seeing my weight as a barometer of my worthiness to experience love for myself, I realised that all of the parameters around loving myself fully were set by ME. The only thing getting in my own way was my own big (and beautiful) arse!

So I did a painful, nausea-inducing exercise that made me realise how many conditions I had set around my own happiness, and I invite you to do it, too. (I know. I sold that really well didn't I? It was the 'nausea-inducing' bit that hooked you, right?)

Exercise 14
GIVE THYSELF A FREAKIN' BREAK!

Answer the following questions (and be honest with yourself):

1. What are the five main things preventing you from loving yourself completely?

2. If you could change any five things about yourself, inside or out, what would they be? And why?

3. If you were told that none of the things you've listed in the previous two questions could be changed, could you love yourself despite them?

The big aha moment for me during this exercise came when I realised that none of the things that stopped me from loving myself were things that would stop me from loving another person. So why should the parameters for loving myself be any different?

They're not, they're exactly the same, and you're just harder, meaner and more critical of yourself than others because you know you're stuck with you for life. If you spoke to someone else the way you spoke to yourself, they'd be out of there in a heartbeat. But the fact that the only person you can't abandon in your life is you *should* be your number-one reason for wanting to accept and love yourself right now, unconditionally.

You're wasting your energy by not loving yourself

I spoke about wasted energy output in Chapter 5. When it comes to our self-love and self-worth, we spend so much energy on decreasing rather than boosting it, and half the time we're not even aware that we're doing it!

By now you know that focusing all of your awareness on something increases its vibrational frequency. When it comes to critiquing ourselves, we're all pretty freaking good at it. We focus our thoughts, feelings AND actions on supporting and increasing those low self-esteem vibes. Madness!

Up until about two years ago, I spent countless hours a day staring at my thighs in the mirror. I'd look at them from all angles; pull at my inner thighs, push my saddlebags up, turn around to see my butt, lift up my butt cheeks, and then do the exact same pull, push, rotate and lift—just in a different mirror in the house.

I was never satisfied by my reflection. If I looked good, I put it down to a good mirror or perfect lighting, not a real representation of me. If I looked terrible, I prayed it was because the mirror was bad or the lighting was awful. Basically, I didn't trust any reflection of myself ever, which begs the question what was the point of looking in the goddamn mirror in the first place?

Every time I put myself through this ordeal, it made me feel depressed and frustrated. My internal dialogue would pipe up, 'You're so unattractive. Who could love thighs like that?' Inevitably, I'd cap things off by tumbling down an online wormhole, searching for thigh exercises, non-surgical fat reduction, cellulite creams … and before I knew it, another afternoon had disappeared.

So much wasted energy! It makes me so mad to think about all that time I spent bathing in a low vibration. Staring in the mirror wasn't doing anyone any favours. There was literally no point to it whatsoever. Nada!

Another energy-wasting trap we are conditioned to fall into is the comparison trap. And do you know who the biggest villain in this story is? Social freaking media.

How much energy have you wasted scrolling through Instagram and Facebook, comparing yourself to influencers, fitspo models and celebrities? I'm not even going to spend a lot of time on this because I know that you know it's not real life. You're way smarter than that! I am, too, but it still doesn't stop me from falling into the Instagram vortex every now and then. All I'm going to say is filters, lighting, editing software and a thousand photos taken to find the one.

Right now, I want you to put down this book (just make sure you come back) and do a little exercise. Go through all of your social accounts and unfollow any people who make you feel less joy. Because I'm pretty sure Mark Zuckerberg's plan when he invented Facebook was not to make people feel shit about themselves (oh wait, actually, now that I think about it, that was exactly his plan. Okay, screw Zuckerberg!).

Exercise 15
IDENTIFYING THOSE ENERGY SUCKERS

Let's start by dividing your life into four main areas (feel free to divide further if you need to).

1. Physical appearance
2. Relationships
3. Career
4. Finances

In terms of self-love, self-worth and self-esteem, where are you wasting your energy in these areas of your life? Ask yourself what counterproductive thoughts, feelings and actions are preventing you from having higher vibrations in these areas?

The point is to cut the comparisons! Trust me, the less energy you waste on comparing yourself to edited images of someone else's fake life, the better.

Time for another fun—well, not fun, but necessary—exercise (see opposite) to determine where else you are wasting your energy.

Watch out for being a mirror

A sure-fire way to know if someone has low self-esteem is to watch how they interact with other people. The bullies, narcissists and Judgey McJudges of this world are all reflecting their low vibes out to deflect from themselves, and this is something to watch for in yourself. Do you judge people by the clothes they wear? Where they live? Who they date? What they do? The tone of their voice?

I used to walk into a yoga class and scan it to see if I was the curviest one in there. I'd feel relieved whenever there was a girl with more junk in her trunk than me. What. The. Actual. That thought pattern is so horrible, and the only purpose it served was to lower my own vibration.

Now when I walk into a room (and I have some time up my sleeve), I do a quick scan and say something complimentary about everyone (internally, of course, I mean externally would be nice but time-consuming and probs creepy). Because when we're negative about others, all it's really doing is just revealing our own insecurities. So the next time you catch yourself judging someone, take a breath and ask yourself why this might be happening. Is there some insecurity in you that is bubbling up right now? What is that about? Are there any steps you can take to address it?

Take the high road, and the universe will be waiting for you

You know what finally stopped me from checking my thighs out twenty times a day in the mirror and searching for someone fatter than me in every room? It was the realisation that when I chose *not* to follow the trail of insecurity, the flow of energy between the universe and me was a lot clearer. Let's use money as an example.

If you're trying to manifest money, but your inner voice is saying things like 'I don't deserve it' or if you're telling people, 'Oh, I'm no good with money' and you aren't taking action to save money, well then the universe is going to be bloody confused. It's going to think, 'She wants to manifest money, but she believes she doesn't deserve it *and* she doesn't know what to do with it? I'm not giving this woman a cent!' That universe, she a diva!

Self-loathing, whether focused on your looks, your finances, your relationships or other area of your life, blocks the clear channel between you and the universe. It's as simple as that, and this is the reason I keep telling you that until you get self-love sorted, you're going to struggle with manifestation.

APPLYING THE MANIFESTATION EQUATION TO IMPROVE YOUR SELF-LOVE AND SELF-WORTH

We spent the first half of this book learning about the theory of the Manifestation Equation, so we best get around to putting it into practice. The good news is you can absolutely manifest a deeper self-love and a higher self-worth, but this does require some dedication and breaking of old habits.

Before we start, I want to be clear that self-love doesn't mean having to always be satisfied with yourself and never looking to improve. You can absolutely want to lose weight, but it needs to come from a place of love rather than a place of fear. Less punishing your body through exercise and more exercising because it makes you feel fabulous. Less burning yourself out at work for that promotion, even though you're not sure you're worthy of it, and more studying something you love that will improve your chances of getting that promotion because you know it will bring you joy, and you bloody deserve some joy. See the difference?

Okay, let's do this!

Thoughts

Remember when we discussed how the majority of the thoughts we have aren't even true? Well, the thoughts we have about ourselves are usually the most false of all.

Many of the thoughts that are on a constant loop in our head are preposterous lies, things that would sound ridiculous if we said them out loud, and we most certainly wouldn't *under any circumstances* say them about other people. But among all of those mean and nasty thoughts is a bunch of limiting beliefs.

As I mentioned in Chapter 2, when it come to our own worthiness, limiting beliefs are perhaps the biggest culprit. When you think you're not worthy, deserving, special enough, kind enough or smart enough, you immediately limit yourself and your potential. If you're constantly telling yourself that you can't, well, my dear, the universe is going to agree with you—you are leaving it no other choice.

When our self-worth is low, our thoughts tend to follow similar patterns. See if you can identify with any of the following ways of thinking.

Negative Nancy/Nigel: You choose to focus on an insignificant negative that was part of a much larger positive. For example, you're delivering a 30-minute keynote speech at a very large corporate event. Your boss is in the crowd, so if you do well, it could mean a promotion. Fifteen minutes in, and the crowd is loving it. They laugh at the funny bits, they nod in recognition, and you even get a wink of approval from your boss in the front row. Then, suddenly, you stumble on a word and forget your next cue. For all of 5 seconds you shuffle through your cards to find your spot again. The time is up and the crowd goes wild with applause. A few people even stand up. But when you walk offstage, all you can think about is that fumble. You berate yourself for it, and that little insignificant slip-up becomes the filter through which you now see yourself as a public speaker.

If I'm not the best, I'm the absolute worst: If you can't do something perfectly, then why do it all? Can you relate to this? I can. I have this thing where I pretty much only do things that I excel at and avoid at all costs things I'm not good at (team sports, for example). It's something I've really had to pull myself up on because the thing is, when I do fail at something, I immediately tell myself I'm a failure. Not just someone who isn't good at clay pinch-pot making (I'm terrible, can't even make an ashtray), but an all-round failure. Full stop. Because sometimes when we feel down about a certain area of our life, we use it as a sweeping statement for our whole life, and our thoughts begin to reflect this.

But potentially the most damning thing about the perfection trap is that you place too much emphasis on being 'perfect' at the things you *are* good at, so now there's a tonne of pressure on you to NEVER fail at those things. But failure is part of learning and growing. A fear of failure can limit your life experiences, keep you from coming into contact with amazing new people and stifle your potential to evolve.

Labelling: Aka the little sister of the thought pattern above. I'm useless. I'm boring. I'm hopeless. (Such sweeping statements, sweetie!) Labelling is when we call ourselves names based on a situational event, allowing it to define us.

Should do this. Must do that: Setting yourself parameters isn't only a problem when it comes to manifestation, it is also bad news when it comes to thoughts. We set standards for ourselves based on fabricated data. We tell ourselves things like I should weigh fifty-five kilos; I must have this career to be considered successful; I shouldn't wear that dress; I must save $10,000 by the end of the year. SAYS WHO? Who are all these shoulds and musts for? Running your thoughts like this sets you up for disappointment and failure. If the standards you set for yourself are too rigid, your self-esteem will take a battering if you don't quite achieve them.

Reading minds: He thinks I'm a bimbo. She thinks I'm fat. They hate spending time with me. Many of us get caught in the trap of assuming someone thinks a certain way about us with zero evidence that they do.

Catastrophising: Do you always predict the worst-case scenario? For example, your friend doesn't call when they said they would. They either hate you or they've crashed their car and died.

Predicting the future: I'll never finish this project; I'll embarrass myself at the party; no one will like me at my new job. We all are guilty of playing the role of fortune teller when it comes to our own lives, but you know by now that predicting a negative outcome is what will ultimately be the catalyst for its creation.

THE 'CHALLENGE YOUR THOUGHTS' TOOLKIT

Now that you can see the different ways in which your thoughts can manifest and lower your self-worth and self-esteem, the trick is not to cease having them, but instead to challenge them when you recognise them.

Recognise and label. As soon as I have a negative thought, I recognise it and label it as negative, then I let it go. Just because you have had the thought doesn't mean you need to indulge it. This simple technique brought me such freedom. Trying not to have those negative thoughts was exhausting (and near impossible) but recognising them and labelling them made them less debilitating, and I found it easier to let them go.

Stop! A trick that many of my clients enjoy is a more forceful approach to a negative thought, one that I like to call stopping it in its tracks. If you observe a negative thought, stop it in its tracks by yelling STOP! If there's no one around, I encourage you to say it out loud, but you're going to look bonkas if you're around fellow humans, so thinking it loudly works, too.

What are the chances? This is particularly helpful for those catastrophising and future predicting thoughts. Challenge yourself on those negative predictions: what are the chances you'll never actually finish this project? What are the chances that you'll be evicted for being one week late with the rent? Go through the odds in your head as objectively as possible, and you'll soon realise that the chances of your future predictions coming true are pretty low.

Lawyer that thought. If you love courtroom dramas as much as I do, then you'll probably quite enjoy this opportunity to cross-examine your own thought. Don't just let a negative thought get away with wreaking havoc on your emotions, ask it questions like, 'What evidence do you have to support this?' 'Would anyone else be able to corroborate the validity of this thought?' And, my personal favourite, 'Are you willing to swear under oath that this thought is, indeed, true?'

Is this thought worth your energy? The majority of the time, the answer will be no, so you know what to do ... STOP! Remember, the aim is not to *never* have the thoughts. Instead, hold the intention of challenging them when they come up and determining whether or not the thoughts have any legs. If not, let them go.

Feelings

Guilt, shame, anger, embarrassment, pride and anxiety are feelings often associated with low self-worth. But a lot of the time we can feel these things without being able to pinpoint the specific incident that has triggered them.

Challenging the thoughts behind your feelings is a great place to start. Often, recognising a thought as false can be enough to make you realise the accompanying feeling carries no weight.

We have the ability to access each and every feeling we desire whenever we want to. There doesn't need to be a reason or a goalpost we

Exercise 16
LOVE YO'SELF

Start by answering this question: how do you want to feel about yourself?

Now let's get more specific. Go through the same four (or more) main areas we divided your life into in Exercise 15 when you were identifying where you were wasting your energy.

1. Physical appearance
2. Relationships
3. Career
4. Finances

Now that you've identified where you were wasting energy in each of those areas, replace that wasted energy with positive energy. How do you desire to feel in each of the areas listed above?

Just like in the High Vibrations Meditation (page 73), can you feel each of those feelings right now in this moment without physically changing a single thing about yourself?

If you feel resistance behind this exercise, I urge you to drop the negative stories around each area of your life. For example, if you want to feel happiness, joy and pride around your appearance, stop the internal voice from saying, 'But I don't feel those things,' or 'I'll feel those things when I'm this dress size or that weight.' Just feel the feelings separate from the story, right now in this very moment.

have to reach first. Loving yourself can be as simple as feeling the vibration of love in each and every cell of your body. By doing this, not only are you raising your own love frequency, but you're also attracting similar love frequencies towards you.

When it comes to my body woes, all I truly desire is to feel at peace. No more battling, no more frustration, no more punishment, guilt or shame, just peace. So when I feel myself spiralling and heading towards a round of pull, push, rotate and lift, instead I close my eyes and tap into the feeling of peace permeating through each and every cell in my body.

Actions

We're halfway through the Manifestation Equation now. We've stopped the thoughts in their tracks, labelled them for what they are (mostly fiction), and made them defend themselves against a hard line of questioning. We've also replaced those feelings of guilt, shame, anxiety, etc. with the more positive feelings we desire to feel about ourselves. So now it's time to walk the talk (or walk the thoughts and feelings).

In order for your self-worth to truly improve for the better, your actions need to reflect the internal changes you're making. When you take conscious action for your own betterment, you can't help but feel self-empowered.

Here are seven actionable steps that you can start taking today to manifest deeper self-love and higher self-worth.

1. **Practice authenticity, always.** A huge chunk of your own self-criticism comes from the fear of what other people are going to think about you. But here's a newsflash for you: pretending to be someone you're not to please other people is exhausting and

probably the biggest waste of energy there is. When you can drop the pretense and just be yourself, there is an infinite amount of freedom to be gained.

Authenticity is the fuel for our vibrational frequency. When we are standing proud in the truth of who we are, the universe responds accordingly. It's the channel I referred to earlier—the more aligned you are with the essence of 'you', the clearer that channel becomes.

2. **Say what you mean, and mean what you say.** Do you often want to say no to someone but end up saying yes to avoid hurting their feelings? And then end up feeling shitty? Or do you hold back from telling someone how you're really feeling because you're afraid of their response? Every time you do this, you're moving out of alignment with your own authenticity by prioritising their feelings over your own. Standing up for yourself is an act of self-empowerment, and you don't have to be mean or nasty when doing it, you just need to be firm and decisive.

Like many women, I've always been a bit of a people pleaser, and I hate the idea of someone not liking me. But a couple of years ago, I realised that saying something I didn't mean, or agreeing to something I didn't want to do, meant that I felt an overwhelming sense of resentment, not only towards the other person, but also to myself. What was the point? So I began practising being honest, firm and kind in all of my exchanges—this left me feeling satisfied and meant the other person received the respect of my truth. Win-win.

For example, rather than agree to take on more than I could handle, I might say something like, 'Susan, I understand you need someone to cover your yoga class for you, but I am already teaching ten classes this week and wouldn't feel comfortable about taking any more classes on.'

3. **And don't apologise for it.** Have you seen that Blake Lively and Anna Kendrick movie, *A Simple Favor*? Kendrick's character apologises profusely for everything, even when she has done nothing wrong. Lively's character is constantly pulling her up on it: 'Baby, if you apologise again, I'm going to have to slap the sorry out of you.'

Women do this ALL THE TIME. We over-apologise for things that do not warrant the S-word: Sorry, is this seat taken? I'm so sorry to bother you. I'm sorry you missed your bus this morning. Sorry I couldn't cover your yoga class, Susan. We often use this word as a cushion for other people's feelings or to smooth over saying what we mean, fearing something might be misconstrued or, god forbid, someone might think we aren't nice. But apologising for something you're not guilty of means you're subconsciously taking the blame for a crime you didn't commit, and this takes you out of alignment with your own authenticity.

I've had to be very conscious of refraining from apologising to potential clients when I can't fit their projects into my calendar, or if I simply don't want to take on the work. Having a full calendar is not something to apologise for—it's almost as if saying sorry got confused with being polite. I would use the S-word all the time when replying to emails about my availability. Now, I remove all of the apologies before I hit send.

When you save your sorries for those times that you're actually apologising for a wrongdoing, they hold much more weight and meaning.

4. **Watch how you talk about yourself.** Be super wary of labels when describing yourself to other people. And by this I mean saying things like, 'Oh yeah, I'm like that because I'm a Gemini' or 'I'm not great at relationships because my parents had an ugly divorce' or 'I'm a terrible decision-maker'. Labels are some of the greatest blindfolds and invisibility cloaks around—they make excellent cover-ups and excuses under which we can hide our real selves.

Exercise 17
MASKS AND LABELS

Grab your journal and have a think about how you describe yourself to others.

Write down some of the labels you've given yourself.

What are some of the masks you hide behind?

5. **Be kind to yourself when you make mistakes.** Without mistakes there is no growth, so instead of being hard on yourself when you slip up, start looking for the lessons there are to be learned. Mistakes are only an issue when you continue to make the same one over and over again. Punishing yourself or defining your worth by the mistakes you make only serves to lower your vibration. I check in with myself regularly to see if there is anything that I could have done 'better', and then I look at ways to improve next time. Because I'll let you in on a little life hack I discovered: there are no mistakes! Every 'wrong' turn we make was predestined to put us back on the 'right' path.

6. **Take responsibility for your actions.** This is your chance to step up. We touched on this in Chapter 5, but it bears repeating. Responsibility is your ability to respond, so when things are not going your way, what are you going to do about it? Instead of blaming others and looking for external reasons for why a situation went a certain way, can you accept that YOU are the creator of your own future, and everything that happens to you is because of your action (or lack of action)? Once I started realising that even my most harrowing experiences happened because of my own actions and taking responsibility for that rather than trying to blame someone (read: anyone) else, I actually started to feel super empowered.

    This also goes for actions that affect other people. I was taught from a very young age that admitting when you're wrong is nothing to be ashamed of. If it turns out I'm not right about something (and I mean, this rarely happens), I'm the first to admit it. This surprises a lot of people I get into confrontations with. If something I've said or done warrants an apology, I'll give one; if it doesn't, I'll say something like, 'I can see your point of view. I misunderstood and you're absolutely right.' No sorry in sight!

7. **Receive and give compliments.** Another quality instilled into me from a very young age by my mum was to accept compliments gracefully. Being sincerely thankful will not be misconstrued for pride or vanity, but what it will do is send a clear message to the universe that you believe you're worthy of those compliments.

    Too often, our instinct is to play the compliment down or reject it entirely, but my mum always told me that it's disrespectful to the person dishing out the compliment not to accept it with grace. And if we reject it, we're essentially rejecting all of the good vibrations attached to it. Keep that in mind next time someone tells you how radiant you look.

Exercise 18
ACCEPTING COMPLIMENTS

See if you can accept every compliment given to you this week. All you have to do is say thank you. You don't have to give one back in exchange, but do dish out compliments if you feel like giving one. Compliments make people feel good, and I know that giving them makes me feel just as good as receiving them.

Individually, these actions might seem small or insignificant, but cumulatively they represent you and how you show up in the universe. We are the action we take based on our thoughts and our feelings, and when we can align these thoughts and feelings with a deep sense of self-love and a high sense of self-worth, I'm telling you ANYTHING is possible.

Faith

Believing in yourself means having strong faith in your own ability to make decisions guided by your intuition (which we spoke about in Chapter 6). The more you use your intuition, the stronger your sense of self becomes, so strengthen your intuition by using it in each and every moment.

From now, when you find yourself in a moment of self-doubt or self-loathing, instead of reaching for answers externally, try sitting quietly with yourself, even if this makes you feel uncomfortable. Discomfort is only energy and vibrations, and it WILL move through you, I promise.

Exercise 19
PEACEFUL BREATHING

☾ Bring your awareness to a problem in need of a solution.

☾ Close your eyes and tune in to your natural breath.

☾ Place both hands gently over your belly. Notice the inhale, the pause at the top, the exhale and the pause at the bottom.

☾ Slowly begin to deepen the breath, feeling the subtle sensation of your hands rising and falling with each inhale and each exhale.

☾ Tap into the feeling of peace. With each inhale and exhale breath, feel peace slowly flood through every cell of your body. Stay here for as long as you need.

☾ Once peace has become your vibration (and it will if you keep breathing), then you'll have a clear channel to your inner guidance.

Intuitively, what do you believe is the next step forward? Without asking for confirmation from someone else, and without googling it or taking a poll on your Instagram stories, can you have faith in your own choices and faith that you are being supported by the all-knowing, all-seeing universe?

Whenever I am confused or having trouble making a decision, I take all the variables out of the equation. I remove other people's opinions, my own expectations, financial factors, fear, past experiences and anything that might cloud or impact the clear channel to my intuition. Instead, I choose to focus on what will bring me peace and joy.

Rose had been battling a severe eating disorder for three years when she came to see me for manifestation mentoring. I was very clear with her from the start of the six-month program that I was not going to help her with her disordered eating, and that in order for us to work together she would need to see a psychologist as well. She agreed, and we began our program.

Rose's inability to manifest what she wanted in life stemmed from her low self-esteem, of which her eating disorder was a by-product. I started our first session by letting Rose know that she was enough exactly where she was in her life right now. Eating disorder and all, she was enough. These simple words transformed her more than I could have ever imagined. She didn't know that. Nobody had ever told her that she was enough, and she had certainly never said it to herself.

What happened next was inspiring. Instead of turning to food for comfort and validation, Rose began tuning into her intuition. Rather than punishing herself with exercise, Rose began taking rest days as a form of self-love. And even though we never discussed healing her disordered eating directly, she began to use the Manifestation Equation in the moments that would ordinarily lead up to a binge.

She would ask herself if the thoughts she was having were true in that moment. Then she'd ask, 'How will I *feel* if I choose to binge? How will I *feel* if I choose not to? Can I tap into *that* feeling right now?' If Rose chose to binge, she did not berate herself for it, but rather viewed it as a lesson for how she might better navigate the situation in the future.

Rose is still battling her inner demons and by no means has healed completely, but she now has an unwavering faith that she can get over each individual road bump as it arises. She believes, without a doubt, that she has the full support of the universe and that she can and will fully recover.

Self-love and valuing your own self-worth is paramount to successful manifestation, but it isn't something that you will master in one day. It is an ongoing process and evolution of your soul, something you will need to constantly check in with and revisit throughout your life. The wisdom of this chapter is that self-love is *not* about self-improvement, or looking for the answers externally. It's a deep dive into self and into practising self-acceptance of where and who you are in each and every moment.

Recognising the difference between self-improvement and self-acceptance is one of the most liberating breakthroughs you can have. Understanding each of them and being able to distinguish between them will absolutely transform the way you manifest.

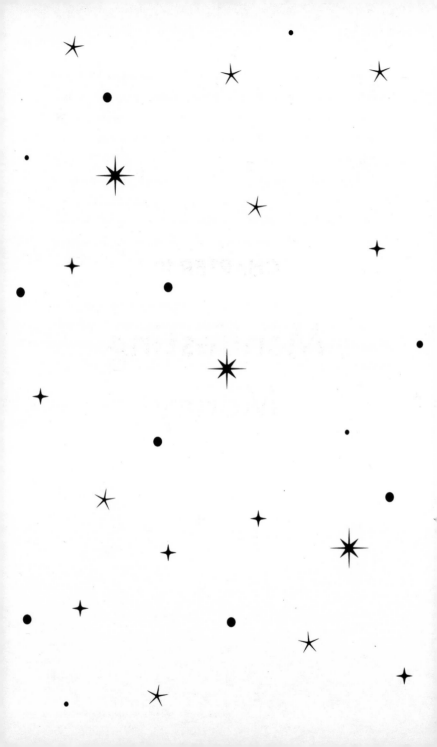

CHAPTER 10

Manifesting Money

My money story used to read like this:

> *I'm a terrible saver. I can't afford a holiday. There's never*
> *enough. I'm always in debt. I'll never be able to afford that.*
> *I'll never make that much money in my industry. I'm broke.*
> *Being an adult is so expensive …*

On and on and on it went.

The story I'd created in my head about my relationship with money governed both my internal and external dialogue and, unbeknown to me at the time, this story I'd subconsciously crafted with permanent ink was painting a pretty bleak financial future for me.

I avoided paying bills. Heck, I even avoided opening them. I'd just leave them sitting on the coffee table. My logic was that if I didn't pay them and still had the money in my account, it would somehow make me feel wealthier—it didn't. What doing this did give me was a bad credit rating (and anxiety). I had zero clues about what my outgoings were, and I never bothered to look at what was coming in. I just knew how much I had, and hoped and prayed that it would be topped up before my rent was due.

When you're working for yourself, money management can be tricky, especially when you don't know where the next job is coming from. But it didn't matter whether I was on a decent salary working a full-time job or freelancing with no idea where my next client would be coming from because my bank account still resembled a giant sieve either way.

It didn't matter how much money went in, it would just fall straight back out again.

I would often look around at my friends and wonder how they afforded the holidays that they took or the cars and apartments that they had. I would find myself consumed by other people's financial situations and constantly comparing them to my own. Even when I was working full-time in the publishing industry on the exact same salary as my colleagues, I couldn't understand why I always had $1.65 in my account before payday and they were booking summers in Europe.

As much as I was consumed by money, I also didn't like discussing it. It made me feel uncomfortable. In fact, it terrified me, mainly because I didn't know what to do with it. I was never taught how to manage it, or even that it was something that you should manage. 'I'm just not good with money' was something I would regularly say, as if I was born that way and destined to remain that way forever.

When I began working with manifestation, my finances were the first thing I tried to apply the Manifestation Equation to. Easy, right? Change my thoughts and shift my vibrations around money, start taking some conscious action steps to start saving and managing my money better, and trust that as sure as money would go out it would also come back in again. But the problem was I couldn't get past my thoughts. I had countless limiting beliefs around money, and they were all built around scarcity and never having enough. Where had these limiting beliefs come from?

Growing up, I never went without, but I certainly didn't have the same lifestyle that many of my schoolfriends had. An only child of divorced parents, I lived with my single mother, a small-business owner, in a modest (read: small) yet happy and comfortable home in a decent Sydney suburb. On the weekends I'd stay with my corporate exec dad, stepmum and half siblings in a larger, yet still modest and charming home in an arguably more affluent Sydney suburb.

Many of my private-school friends grew up in homes that you could comfortably refer to as mansions, and they were gifted European luxury cars at the age of sixteen. I remember that when it was decided that I would go to a private girls' school in Sydney's eastern suburbs, my dad said something along the lines of, 'These girls are going to have more than you. You will feel inadequate at times, but we just don't have the same kind of money as them. Do you understand?' At least this is how that sentence stuck in my mind. And bless him, Dad was trying to do what all fathers want to do for their daughters: protect them. But my twelve-year-old brain immediately took that statement and used it to create a divide between 'me' and 'them'.

Neither of my parents really spoke about money. I knew Dad had more than Mum, and I knew Mum had to work hard to make ends meet, but she never whinged about it. She would tell me when we couldn't afford something, and I would plead like most children do. Sometimes she would cave and other times she would apologise for not being able to buy me whatever insignificant thing I didn't think I could live without. But our discussions around money never went further than that. If I needed a considerable amount of money, I was told to ask my father. Now I love my dad with every single cell in my body and with my whole heart, but he can be a scary man when it comes to discussing finances, especially to a twelve-year-old.

My father had arrived in Australia from South Africa in 1980 with his first wife and my two half brothers, and in a matter of years had climbed many a corporate ladder in the commercial retail sector and was very successful. At the peak of his career, he was sitting pretty at the top. Unlike Mum, who dabbled in money conversations, Dad never spoke about it. He had money. He wasn't tight with it and he looked after all of us, but it was never, ever discussed.

Whenever I had to broach the subject with him because I needed money for something, I became stricken with fear. I'm not sure if this was self-inflicted or warranted, but it always felt like I was heading into a board meeting to do a business transaction (at the age of twelve), not asking a parent for some cash. I would need to have all of the details of said transaction clearly defined before going into the 'meeting'—what the money was for, how much I would need and when I would need it by. I mean, these are all very reasonable questions, but because we never spoke about money, it felt unfamiliar and daunting. And these emotions of fear and lack around money became the vibrations associated with money that stuck with me through my young adult life.

It's funny now, looking back on it as a woman in her mid-thirties, because my dad is probably the *least* scary person I know. He is also the only seventy-year-old I know who still splurges on clothes, gadgets and Japanese gardening tools on a regular basis. But the thing about growing up is that our minds and consciousness are just beginning their journey. They never stop evolving, but in our infancy they're impressionable and malleable, and consequently insignificant, off-the-cuff remarks can become the beliefs we take into our adult lives.

I wish my parents had sat me down and taught me what the f*ck to do with money. How to save it, how to spend it, what to invest it in, how to value it … I wish school had made it part of the curriculum. Why didn't they? They taught me how to deposit it in a Dollarmites account, but the conversation didn't go further than that. It's nobody's fault; it's just part of our growth as humans. My parents probably thought not talking about money was doing me a service. Perhaps they didn't know how to manage it themselves, who knows? It doesn't actually matter.

Money, like everything in the universe, is just energy. Nobody is more or less deserving of it. It's not good or bad. It is a piece of paper, metal or plastic that one day a very long time ago had value placed upon it, and not just monetary value but our own personal values and belief systems.

TIME TO APPLY THE MANIFESTATION EQUATION TO MONEY

Now that you have a better idea of how these negative stories around money can form in our impressionable young heads and trip us up later as adults, it's time to roll up your sleeves and do some work. If you've got your finances totally sorted and are sitting pretty on top of piles of savings and investments, go you! You're ahead of the game. But if some (or most) of my money story rings true for you, don't worry because you can change that story. Working through this chapter will help you grow no matter what your current story is. Ready? Money, we're coming for you.

Thoughts

If you want to start manifesting financial freedom, the first thing you need to do is take a good, hard look at your own money story. We've all got one—they are penned by our own thoughts and limiting beliefs around money since we were old enough to know that five cents could buy us a red frog at the corner store (those were the days).

You've heard my old money story, now it's time to tell yours. This next exercise might feel icky, but that's the point! If you want to write a new story, you need to be clear about why money has been a struggle up until now. If money isn't an issue for you, you'll still find this exercise useful.

Exercise 20
GETTING REAL ABOUT
YOUR MONEY STORY

In your journal, reflect on your money story as it stands today.
Start by using these questions as prompts:

1. How would you describe your relationship
   with money?

2. What are your current belief systems around money?

3. When you were a kid, how did the adults
   around you behave with and about money?

4. What stories were you told about money
   by your parents?

5. Were you ever taught what to do with money?

6. What do you believe lies in your financial future?

Hopefully, answering each of these questions will give you
a little perspective and a better understanding of why you
interact with money the way that you do.

Now let's take this one step further. If you had to summarise
your current money story in one paragraph, what would that
look like? This was mine:

Money terrifies me. I don't really understand how to manage
money properly, therefore I relinquish any kind of responsibility
around it. I spend it just as fast as I make it and choose to
ignore bills and financial commitments. I'll never be able
to afford to buy a home, and the concept of a mortgage just
seems burdensome and something I would never want. I have

*a money threshold. I can only make so much money and then
that's it. My career choice has limited my earning potential.
I should have become an investment banker, or perhaps I should
just marry one? I have so much debt, and I'll never be able to pay
it off. I'm such an idiot. How did I get in so much debt?*

Now that your current money story is written down in black and white, can you identify where your beliefs around money originated and why they're preventing you from manifesting financial freedom?

As discussed earlier, sometimes being aware of a limiting belief is enough to shift it, other times it requires a little more digging. Now that we have a basic foundation in the form of your thoughts and limiting beliefs around money, it's time to have a look at the fuel behind them: the feelings and vibrations keeping you stuck in a state of lack and scarcity.

Feelings

When we feel a certain way about something (or someone), we create a vibration around it. And if we apply this to money, according to the Law of Vibration if we are constantly operating from a place of scarcity, we are going to attract more scarcity towards us. Exercise 21 on the following page looks at the feelings fuelling your current money story. Taking the time to examine these feelings is important because you can't change those all-important vibrations without addressing these.

Exercise 21

FEELING YOUR CURRENT MONEY STORY

Read through the money story you wrote in Exercise 20, and identify each one of the feelings that you currently associate with money. Write these feelings down in your journal.

As you begin listing these feelings, you will probably notice that more and more of them begin to surface during this process. Write those ones down, too. Writing your feelings down is part of the releasing process. Remember, we don't just want to *think* the feelings, we want to *feel* the feelings (even the ones we no longer wish to identify with), so we can allow them to move through us.

The feelings that came up for me while writing my old money story were fear, lack, irresponsibility, hopelessness, anxiety, instability, immaturity, ignorance and frustration.

The feelings that surfaced while I was writing down those emotions were overwhelm, suffocation, paralysis, shame and guilt.

Ooof! Heavy stuff to be carrying in your wallet, right?

See how layered our thoughts and feelings can be? This is why it's important that we take the time to dig deep so we can excavate them, release them and replace them with new vibrations.

YOU are the creator of your future and the author of every single story you tell yourself over and over again. Just as you wrote your original money story, the one you've been running your entire life, you now have the ability to write a new one.

But first, you'll have to decide how you want to *feel* as the protagonist of this new tale.

Exercise 22

MONEY AND THE FUTURE YOU

Without concentrating on the how, why, when, where or what, write down the feelings that you want to experience when it comes to money. Here are some questions to get you started:

☾ How does being debt-free make you feel?

☾ How does it feel to know you'll never have to worry about having enough money again?

☾ How does knowing what to do with money make you feel?

☾ How does it feel to be a rock-star saver with plenty in the bank for a rainy day?

Actions

Before we get to writing your new money story, there's some admin that we need to do. You're probably going to moan about it—I certainly did. But if you want to change your money habits, you've got to get clued in to the finer details about your own money situation first. Exercise 23 is crucial to your evolution. If you long to finally feel good about your money situation (and who doesn't!) please do not skip this step!

CREATE A (REAL!) BUDGET

If you want to understand money, feel calm about your own finances and start raking in the moolah, you need to know the ins and outs (literally) of your own financial situation. There are plenty of (easy and free) tools online that can help you put together a budget, but a pretty simple way to get started is by writing down a few key things ... (Read on!)

Exercise 23
BUDGETING 101

1. **Calculate your monthly income.** This includes every single income stream you have from side hustles, rental properties, babysitting, bake sales, everything! If, like me, you don't have a consistent income because you own your own business or you're a freelancer or contractor, then just use your average income from the last three months as a starting point.

2. **Calculate your monthly expenses.** Split these into different categories.

    ☾ Regular fixed expenses: These are the non-negotiable expenses that you have to pay every month. Things such as rent/mortgage, electricity, insurance, debt repayments, groceries (superfoods count, right?) etc. go in this list.

    ☾ Discretionary expenses: This is fun stuff that you could live without if you had to. Things such as entertainment, eating at restaurants, personal care, clothing, holidays, gym memberships and subscriptions such as Netflix and Spotify go in this category.

    The discretionary expenses are the things you can tighten up on, if you need to (eeep!). And note that grocery shopping can be tightened up, too, if your weekly list tends to be on the long side.

3. **Add any financial milestones you'd like to hit to your discretionary expenses.** For example, if you've got a debt you'd like to pay off, a holiday you're saving for or an emergency savings account you'd like to fund, decide when you'd like to achieve that goal by, then work out how much you'll need to put towards that goal each month in order to

hit it by your target date. Add that number to your monthly discretionary expenses.

4. **Subtract your income from your expenses.** Don't freak out after you do this! Whatever happens at this point, whether you're living within your means or way beyond them, you're already taking the initiative to change things.

5. **Now adjust your expenses accordingly.** The first three steps show you what state your finances are in. Now, before you even consider the intentions that you're about to set to increase your earnings and manifest financial freedom, I want you to show up for, and be present with, your current financial situation. If you need to, make adjustments to your discretionary expenses in order to free up more cash. This might mean having to listen to ads on your music-streaming account, saying no to a few big nights out, or putting your gym membership on hold and doing your exercise outdoors for a few months. Next, make any changes necessary to the financial milestones you've set. This might mean moving back the target date on one of your goals by a few months, or putting off that holiday until next year.

Congratulations! Now you've got a solid starting point to work with.

Disclaimer
I am by no means a financial advisor (like, not even close), but this budgeting exercise is mandatory if you want to start rewriting your money story.

PAY YOUR BILLS (ON TIME)

This action sounds pretty simple, but if you're anything like me (and I have a sneaking suspicion you might be), you probably don't pay your bills until the final notice appears with lots of red lettering and a late payment fee to boot. So let's stop this behaviour, shall we? Prolonging the payment of bills tells the universe that you don't believe that you're going to have more money coming.

I'd better not spend what I have in case there's nothing to replace it with. This was a thought pattern that I had to work hard to break. And truthfully, I still revert to it sometimes when my faith gets tested and I forget that money is just energy and something that works in cycles, just like everything in the universe. Every time I pay a bill and do the right thing, the money comes back in, always.

As a small-business owner, I get frustrated when clients don't pay their invoices on time. Don't they understand that contractors and small-business owners rely on invoices being paid on time for consistent cash flow? When a client who owed me over $5,000 kept ignoring my emails and phone calls over a period of several weeks, I found myself incredibly frustrated by her inability to understand the impact that not receiving that money was having on my business. I was relying on that money being paid on time in order to keep things running, and now here I was falling behind on my own payments because she had failed to meet her obligations.

As I sat there, incredibly frustrated, I went back to basics. If money was simply energy, then I needed to get the cycle moving again. I went through my emails and realised that I had let an invoice to my bookkeeper lapse two days past its due date, not because I didn't have the money, but because I hadn't made it a priority (even though my bookkeeper is *also* a small-business owner). I immediately paid her and, no joke, the very next day my client settled her bill, after me chasing her for weeks. It's energy, people. Just energy.

REMEMBER THAT THE UNIVERSE CAN'T LOG IN TO YOUR BANK ACCOUNTS

When I manifested $20,000 (the first time), my intention was to pay off all of my debt. I set an intention around the specific amount of money I needed to clear my credit cards and student loans, and after months of applying the Manifestation Equation to my intention that $20,000 showed up in my bank account in the form of an unexpected contract job.

Turns out I should have manifested more money because half of that money ended up going towards expenses related to the job, including hiring staff to assist me. The other half went on ... god knows what. In retrospect, I should have logged into my bank account and transferred that money directly onto my credit cards. But I didn't. I was a contractor, and my old money story was still running the show—I was terrified that more money wouldn't come in. So, with those feelings of scarcity pumping through my veins, I held on tightly to the remaining $10,000 and made no effort to lower my debt. And slowly, I watched that money dwindle down to nothing.

The lesson here is that you can absolutely manifest yourself out of debt, but the universe won't pay off your credit card or clear your student loans. YOU have to do that bit. And, full disclosure: I still haven't nailed this aspect of my money story. To this day, I still flip in and out of scarcity and abundance. But this comes down to three things: fear, faith and being human. The only way to get 'better' at this is to try again next time you are given the opportunity. And you will get another one; the universe is good like that.

Faith

You're about to rewrite your money story, but before you do I have a confession to make. To be completely honest, I wrote, deleted and then rewrote this confession a few times—I even questioned whether to include it at all. But this book is a true account of my journey with manifestation, and when I sat down to write it I made a promise to myself that I would inject authenticity into each and every page. No bullshit, just the truth of who I am. So here goes ... (deep breath)

I am still in debt. I have manifested $20,000 twice now. I can manifest money whenever my reserves are getting low, and I can teach you how to do the very same thing. Yet, still, I have a block around money and a resistance to taking the action required to clear my credit cards, pay my taxes on time and build up a savings fund.

As I said, I very easily flip between feelings of scarcity and abundance. I drop into scarcity when I'm in fear about my finances and terrified of where the next client, job or ticket sale will come from. I fall into feelings of not having enough, not being enough, and soon my world begins to reflect this. I revert to old ways of thinking and speaking about money. I hear myself thinking and saying things like, 'I can't afford it' or 'I'll never have enough'. And there's always the fail-safe, 'Everything is so expensive'. But this only happens when I lose my faith.

When I can trust that money is just energy that ebbs and flows like everything else in the universe, and that there is plenty of it in this world, then I very quickly slip back into an abundance mentality and my finances very swiftly reflect that.

Faith will always dull fear, but recognising that you are human and that it's a natural part of your growth and experience to flip between the two states is a very important notion to grasp around the practice of manifestation, no matter what it is you're trying to manifest.

I promised you right at the beginning of this book that this wouldn't be easy, and I also promised you honesty. So here it is, plain and simple: you are not perfect. There are times that you will falter. There are certain things that you will find easier to manifest than others, and other things that you may never really 'master', but that is not failure, that is growth. And sometimes, right before we upgrade and expand, we get tested more than we've ever been tested before. The true practice of faith is to trust in the contraction, in the shadows, in the times we want to just collapse on the bathroom tiles and admit defeat.

The work that I still have to do around money is not to do with bringing it in, that part I've nailed. My shadow work lies around believing in every cell of my body that I'm worthy of it when it arrives, and that there will be 'plenty more where that came from'. This is something I need to practise day to day. I swing between fear and faith constantly, but I love and respect each feeling equally because they make me whole and they make me #human.

Right, now that I've laid all of my (credit) cards on the table and aired my dirty laundry, let's get to rewriting that money story of yours. Shall we?

INTRODUCING YOUR NEW MONEY STORY

When writing your current money story, the one that has kept you stuck, you were hopefully able to identify the thought patterns and limiting beliefs that you have been playing on repeat in your head. You pinpointed exactly where those beliefs originated from, and that may have been enough for you to release them. If not, that's fine, too—you're going to set up some new beliefs around money (even if you don't actually believe them yet), new ways of feeling about money and new action steps to help you manifest more money, and start practising having faith in the cyclical nature of money so you can participate in an effortless dance of non-attachment with money. Sound good?

Exercise 24
FREE-WRITE YOUR WAY
TO YOUR NEW MONEY STORY

Grab your journal and a pen. Go back to the feelings you listed in Exercise 22 to remind yourself of the feelings you desire to feel around money. Similar to the free-writing you did right before setting your intentions, set 10 minutes on a timer and start writing your new money story.

No pausing, no editing, no inhibitions, just write. Inject the feelings that you listed in Exercise 22, as well as positive new statements to replace the old, tired and useless ones. Detail positive and proactive action steps in your new money story. Dream big and with an endless supply of abundance. Remember, don't worry about the specifics or the logistics, just write.

Applying the Manifestation Equation to your new money story

Now that you have the foundation of your new money story thanks to the free-writing exercise, you can dig further into the detail and start manifesting a better relationship with money by applying the Manifestation Equation to your new story. Let's break it down.

THOUGHTS

What are your new thoughts and beliefs around money? They will have surfaced in the free-writing exercise. Set an intention around your finances, and add this to your current list of intentions from Exercise 3 on page 57. You have a new story now, so this intention won't be blocked by old thought patterns and limiting beliefs.

FEELINGS

How does your new money story make you feel? Tap into those feelings daily. You want them to become your new vibration. Whenever you feel yourself falling into fear and scarcity, feel into your new money vibrations and allow them to override the feelings that pull you into your old story.

ACTIONS

Walk around as if your new money story is happening right now. That doesn't mean spending loads of cash on unnecessary items, or shouting rounds to strangers at the bar, it means walking the walk and talking the talk of someone who is good with money, believes there is an endless supply of it, knows that they're financially supported and will know what to do with it when it arrives in their bank account.

Also, quit talking about finances (especially a lack of finances) with other people. Speech gives our thoughts energy, so choose not to give them more power than they already have. And if people around you use language like I can't afford that, this city is so expensive or I'm so broke, don't indulge the conversation. That's their money story, not yours. Subconsciously, you can take on other people's fears as your own; it's how many of your old thought patterns around money were probably formed in the first place. Actively watch out for this!

In each and every moment, take actions that support your money story. Don't think and feel one way and then act in a counterintuitive manner. When money comes your way, think about how the 'new' money story would handle it. When we show the universe that we mean business, it will support us in ways we can't even fathom with our tiny human brains.

FAITH

This whole chapter is focused on helping you build (and in some cases rebuild) a strong, healthy and vibrant relationship with money. Relationships take work, effort, consistent action and faith. They also require respect, gratitude and unconditional love. Can you treat money as your equal, your friend and your ally? Can you work together in harmony, with synergy as a team?

Personally, I have a lot of forgiveness work to do when it comes to my relationship with money. I still hold pockets of resentment for the times I felt screwed over or hard done by financially. My lesson is to stop blaming money as if it is its own entity and start taking responsibility for where I am financially.

Because (broken record alert) money is just energy, and it holds no greater weight or significance energetically than a coconut or a rubber chicken, and neither of these things have the ability to trigger fear and insecurity in me (well, I mean maybe the chicken), so why should money?

When you contemplate the energy of money, as you surely will after all the things you've discovered in this chapter, here are a few wonderful titbits for you to mull over.

★ Think of money as an energetic currency. The energy you place behind it will determine the energy in which it responds. If you treat it well, it's going to treat you like royalty. But if you crumple notes up in your wallet, let your bookkeeping fall behind (#guilty) and throw silver coins you find in the crevices of your couch into the bin because you don't want the extra weight in your wallet, well, money probably won't like you so much.

★ Money, like all energy, requires a clear channel so it can flow through you. If you're tight with your money and scared to loosen your grip on it, it will create a blockage for the flow of energy.

★ Money, like all energetic frequencies, can hear every word you say, so choose your words wisely.

★ Be conscious with your money (but not a tight-arse). Conscious and mindful money exchange rarely gets you into debt. It's when we are mindless and frivolous that we get ourselves into a financial pickle. But don't confuse conscious for frugal—remember that clear channel? It wants you to enjoy your money.

★ When we get paid for work that we have done, it is an exchange of energy. Our energy is exchanged with the energy of money. Ask yourself if you are being fairly remunerated in this energetic exchange. If you aren't, be aware that you may feel resentful about that, and that negative energy will taint the exchange.

★ Just as money isn't good or bad, you are not born good or bad with it. Your choices and actions determine your relationship with money. And you have the freedom to choose abundance over scarcity in every moment.

★ Energy always has a ripple effect. Your conscious effort to improve your relationship with money will impact everyone around you. Imagine the global impact if the collective became more money conscious? It all starts with you.

★ You don't own money! It doesn't belong to you, it belongs to the universe, and it will keep moving in cycles forever and always. Period.

So let's make a vow here and now, together as a collective (and feel free to change this vow up so it feels true for you):

> *I choose faith and abundance in each and every moment.*
> *I am fully aligned with the high vibrational frequencies*
> *of peace, freedom and stability, and have an unwavering*
> *belief in the infinite supply of money.*
>
> *I love money, and money reciprocates this love by flowing*
> *freely, consistently circulating and topping up financial reserves*
> *in ways that best serve me and my highest interest.*
>
> *I give and receive money in equal measure, contributing to the*
> *natural cycles that all energy chooses to move in. I choose to*
> *remain non-attached, confident that money doesn't need me*
> *to grip or resist, but to trust and surrender.*
>
> *Money, I love you and by standing in my truth and authenticity*
> *I have an unwavering faith that I am always fully supported.*

Now go and make friends with money.

CHAPTER 11

Manifesting Love

I've always been equally fascinated and puzzled by love—the indescribable feelings it evokes, the unexplainable actions it provokes. It's a force that often feels outside our own rationale and logical mind; something that enables (and, at times, coerces) us to do things we'd never dream of without it. It sweeps us into states of bliss and ecstasy, and can swiftly plummet us into the deepest and darkest despair. It's the basis of the greatest stories ever told, and the very thing that keeps our planet populated. Holding out for the perfect form of it is what gets us out of bed each and every day. Lust, romance, dependence, flirtation, devotion, mania, unrequited and casual love (is there really such a thing as casual love?) … No matter what form love takes, it leaves us changed in unexpected ways.

To prepare for writing this chapter, I read a lot about love: essays, classic chick-lit, love-over-adversity romance novels, the poetry of the broken-hearted, young adult fiction exploring first-time love, supernatural love, Gothic love and even a thesis on the nature and chemistry of romantic love. I watched classic romantic comedies across various cultures as well as epic love-fuelled sagas before falling into a vortex of documentaries on love-related topics such as arranged marriages, crazed crimes of passion and the love lives of sex workers. I listened to podcast interviews with relationship therapists, philosophers, historians and celebrity couples, and spent countless hours trawling through love-inspired Spotify playlists. But no matter the medium, subject or the genre, they all seemed to arrive at the same conclusion: love is complicated.

I've said I love you to three out of six lovers, but the truth is I've only been in love twice; on some days, I would say only once, and on days of immense clarity (or denial) I've even flirted with the notion of never. But not once have I been devoid of love or not been surrounded by love and felt it running through my veins. Because love, for me as it is for you, is my essence. Not only is love part of our biological human make-up and driven by a collection of chemicals and hormones (which we will dive into), but it also goes beyond that. Love is an intricate layer of contradictory feelings and a deep sense of knowing (which we either listen to or choose to ignore). It is an unexplained familiarity—an energetic and vibrational pull that we can, if we don't understand it, feel powerless against and disconnected from.

In this chapter we'll explore the constructs that shape our perception of love, namely romanticism and the 'Hollywood effect', and we'll also look at the biological symptoms of love in order to examine the notions of chemistry, soulmates and 'the one'. If you've been confusing your love vibrations, we'll look at why that might be and try out a few techniques to help attract more love to your life. We'll also unpack what it means to be *in* love versus what it is to *be* love.

NICHOLAS SPARKS IS JUST NOT THAT INTO YOU

Nicholas Sparks, author of just about every romance book turned movie you've ever seen, knows how to write a fictional character (and cast a hottie) but not a real person. Books and movies are our escape from real life, and consciously making that distinction is of the utmost importance to your manifesting efforts and potential love life. In our conscious mind we know that these stories and people aren't real, but before we know it our subconscious is rewriting every chance encounter with a stranger as a potential plotline.

If I learned anything from successful self-help book turned movie *He's Just Not That Into You*, it's that we are the rule and Hollywood love stories are the exception. They are based on unconventional, exceptional and unlikely circumstances with no laundry, no taxes and no mundane moments in between. The push and pull is entertaining, the declarations of love with boom-box in tow and rain pelting down are romantic, and simple one liners like 'You had me at hello' pluck at our heartstrings, but they're not something we can or should use to measure or mirror the vibration of love.

British philosopher, bestselling author and School of Life co-founder Alain de Botton has written and spoken on the subject of love extensively through his non-fiction book *Essays in Love* and his novels *On Love* and *The Course of Love*. Of all of his musings, I find his take on romanticism and its responsibility for the catastrophising of our relationships to be the most thought-provoking. During de Botton's talk 'On Love' at the Sydney Opera House in 2016, he said:

> We are shaped by the love narratives that we read. We think
> that we love spontaneously and that we're not influenced by
> what we read and what we see. But we are experiencing love
> within a very historical [and] social context ... We are living in
> the era of romanticism [and it] has been a catastrophe for our
> capacity to have good long-term relationships. If we want to
> have a chance of succeeding at love, we will have to be disloyal
> to many of the romantic notions that got us into relationships
> in the first place.

Romanticism was a literary, artistic and philosophical movement that originated in the 18th century and, inadvertently, that movement is responsible for the way you absorb the vibration of love. Everything you've ever read, watched or heard about love has been influenced by the Romantic ideal, which prioritises imagination over reason, intuition over discernment, and feelings over logic. Now to me, this sounds wonderful, but is it a helpful lens for us to view love through? And does it give us an achievable pedestal to put love on?

I *am* a romantic, often to my detriment, and while I'm not holding out for Prince Charming (or Ryan Gosling), I confess there is a part of me that models my idea of romance and worthy love on the 'Hollywood' love-story models, which in the context of this book represent the entertainment business in general (Bollywood, BBC ... I'm looking at you).

You know how it goes: our innocent female protagonist meets one of two types of man: the brooding, rugged, small-town tradesman with a pick-up truck, or the high-flying, charming and chiselled city businessman with a dark past. There is usually a disapproving father or best friend —this adds drama and obstacle—followed by great adversity (or in a really good story, several adversities) that either involves infidelity, miscommunication, illness or, in extreme cases, death. And one way or another, they overcome or grow stronger through these challenges. His loyalty to her is unwavering, he promises to love her forever and protect her always and then they live happily ever after. Roll credits.

My favourite movie of all time is actually a French film called *Love Me If You Dare*. It is a deeply unconventional and dark love story about two best friends who are caught in an intense and never-ending game of dare. As the pranks become more and more dangerous, the pair realise that the game is a way of hiding their true feelings for each other. The love between Julien and Sophie is extreme and tragic, and honestly this movie is completely messed up! But it's also one of the most romantic movies I've ever seen. It ends with them in a loving embrace in the bottom of a well at a construction site while having wet cement poured over them. Because you know, they'll be together forever now … my heart soars thinking about it.

While I would never want a romance that involves a lifetime of childish games and a love that is literally cemented for all of time, I find myself longing for a lover I'd be willing to crawl under wet cement for. I recall a heated argument with an ex-boyfriend in a summer rainstorm. We were walking home, moments away from breaking up; my floral slip clung to my curves, and his white tank and denim cut-offs were completely soaked. We screamed expletives at each other over the pounding of the thunderous rain, and though I was crying on the outside I was giggling on the inside because there I was, living out my own Hollywood moment— caught between two of my favourite fantasies, *The Notebook* (courtesy of Mr Sparks) and the lyrics of Belinda Carlisle's 'Summer Rain'.

Our relationship didn't recover after that night. There was no declaration of love, no symphony-fuelled soundtrack and definitely no happy ending. Yet that moment, for me, got filed away under 'romantic' and 'passionate' in my subconscious because of the cinematic backdrop of the thunderstorm (courtesy of the Hollywood love model). And truth be told, it is a more vivid memory than many of the other, probably sweeter and more authentic moments I've had.

YOUR BRAIN ON LOVE

The rapid heartbeat, the sweaty palms, the shaking knees, the fumbling of words, the invincibility, the euphoria and the emptiness are all actual symptoms of love. And what can often feel like a surge of emotions being emitted straight from the heart is, in fact, a universal human feeling produced by specific chemicals and neurotransmitters in the brain. Romantic or what?

I want to explore the cerebral interpretation of love with you because having an understanding of our physiological reactions during our experience of loving and being loved can be so revealing when it comes to adjusting our vibration around love. And although love and chemistry between two people cannot always be explained in practical terms, I think brain chemistry is a good place to start.

For her book *Why We Love: The Nature and Chemistry of Romantic Love*, anthropologist Helen Fisher worked with a team of scientists to scan the brains of people who had recently fallen madly in love. Through her fascinating findings, she concluded that love can be broken down into three categories—lust, romance and attachment—and within each category there is a set of chemicals and hormones that can be used to characterise love.

Lust is that overwhelming primordial feeling you get when you just want to rip someone's clothes off (in a good way!). The logical and rational mind is abandoned, and you would do anything in that moment to feel instant satisfaction. Lust is ruled by the sex hormones testosterone and estrogen, which drive our sexual desire and our craving for sexual gratification. Lust is unpredictable, does not guarantee romance or attachment, and we can fall in and out of lust with a simple drop in hormones. Think one-night stands, marital affairs and sex droughts.

Romantic love or attraction is linked to the neurotransmitters dopamine, serotonin and norepinephrine. Dopamine and serotonin are both happy hormones (dopamine is also known as the reward hormone), and norepinephrine gets our heart racing and makes our palms sweaty. Attraction involves the pathways of the brain that are responsible for our 'reward' behaviour, which is what essentially gives us that overwhelming feeling of invincibility and euphoria in the early stages of dating someone. You know when you're so in love you can't eat or sleep? Well that's because dopamine and norepinephrine can decrease your appetite and induce insomnia. How about that obsession that you feel with a partner? The incessant daydreaming, the racing thoughts, the constant checks of your phone? Well, Fisher suspects these persistent and involuntary reactions can be linked to low levels of serotonin.

Feelings of attachment are what enable us to progress from fling to long-term relationship, and there are two hormones facilitating these feelings: oxytocin and vasopressin. Oxytocin is often called 'the cuddle hormone' because women release large quantities of it during childbirth and breastfeeding—the time they need to bond with their offspring. Vasopressin is often linked to the paternal instinct. In the context of love, these hormones don't mean we end up feeling attached in a stage-five clinger sense, but rather that we experience a deep sense of belonging to someone, where we feel a calm and comfortable sense of security.

Now I know this all sounds pretty scientific and super unsexy, and you can take it or leave it, but understanding *why* we feel the way we feel can be immensely comforting, at least it is to me. And perhaps I'm a #nerd, but being able to identify the biological symptoms of love helps me understand not only my own behaviour but also my partner's. And as comforting as it is to understand why love can make us feel so goddamn good, it is also helpful to know why it can plummet us into the depths of despair.

We experience surges of dopamine in both good and bad situations. In fact, dopamine has been extensively studied when it comes to addiction. When we are attracted to someone, the same regions of our brain light up as when an addict takes cocaine, and the withdrawal experience from a drug or from an ex-lover can be equally debilitating and extreme. That feeling of not being able to comprehend a life without them, that's dopamine in overdrive!

But are we powerless to control these chemical and hormonal releases? In a sense, yes. They are part of an involuntary physical reaction, but romantic love is so much more than biology. Anyone who has experienced a deep sense of love knows that it comes hand-in-hand with a complex mixture of thoughts, feelings and actions, not to mention a whole host of variables that get thrown into the mix courtesy of the human being you happen to be in love with!

And while neuroscience might be able to explain why we have certain physiological reactions when we fall in lust or in love or become attached to someone, why are these chemicals and hormones only triggered by certain individuals?

Do we choose who we fall in love with?

Anthropologists and psychologists explain why we feel chemistry with another person by pointing to factors such as attraction, intrigue, our ability to effectively communicate with them, shared interests and spiritual connection, and even similarities in physical appearance. Freud even claimed that we fall in love with people who are mirror images of our ideal self (hello, narcissism!), but I don't believe chemistry can be summed up as easily as this.

Way back in the chapter on feelings, when I introduced you to the Law of Vibration, we discussed that feeling of 'vibing' with someone. Chemistry is essentially (or at least initially) that matching vibration. It's the feeling of alignment, synchronicity and familiarity with another person that cannot be explained or understood on paper.

I met Beau when I was twenty-one and he was twenty-five. Initially, there was no attraction—I actually found him kind of irritating, but there was an unexplained familiarity that I couldn't resist. Without being super clear on how it happened (because, irritating), the two of us formed a friendship. We laughed A LOT, our conversations always flowed and at group gatherings we bounced off each other with our matched wit and intellectual smarts. He demonstrated immense loyalty, was always genuinely interested in what I was doing and what I had to say, and I was mesmerised by his blue eyes, superhero-level problem-solving skills and undivided attention. Slowly a unique and indescribable bond began to form.

We would have sexless sleepovers (at my insistence, not from his lack of trying) after long, boozy nights out with friends. In the mornings I'd suggest he not stay over again (even though I never slept better than when he was by my side). He wasn't my type, we had little in common, and in the daytime, with no alcohol, I struggled to get my head around the idea of an 'us'. Everything in my logical mind told me this was not the guy for me, but we couldn't stay away from each other. It was as if there was an energetic force pulling us together that neither of us could resist, even if we wanted to. When we finally succumbed to our lustful urges, things got complicated.

He was fresh out of an intense and long relationship that had left him raw, and that relationship still held a big piece of his heart. I had just been humiliated by a boyfriend who preferred the company of prostitutes to me. Between us, with our baggage in tow, we danced a six-month-long 'I can't do this but I need you' tango until one of us called it quits. I can't remember who. (It was him.)

Having chemistry with someone and feeling an alignment of vibrations doesn't necessarily equal a happy ending. Exhibit Beau. Yet it's something we won't compromise on when looking for a potential partner. I can tell when I feel energetically aligned with someone, be they a potential lover or the postman, because of the way my body *feels* around them. I instantly feel at ease, words flow easily, I don't fidget, I feel grounded and I get a real sense of being 'home'. People often describe this as a sense of familiarity. But where does this sense of the familiar come from? The whimsical part of me that is tuned in to the fifth dimension wants to say it's a sweet remembering of past lifetimes together, but many psychologists and psychoanalysts will argue that it is a familiarity stemming from childhood–from your parents, old wounds, childhood friends, etc. Could this sense of deep knowing come from an association or memory of something you've already experienced and imprinted in your cells? While I see elements of validity in this theory and can even relate to it on a personal level (I've definitely dated men who share the emotionally reserved qualities of my father), I believe that indescribable feeling of the familiar is a sure indication that you've encountered a soul connection.

REDEFINING SOULMATE

The topic of soulmates is vast and well argued, and there are many different schools of thought. I encourage you to do your own research and feel into what resonates with you. For the purposes of this book and passing on the teachings of manifestation, I will share with you my personal experience and understanding of what I believe a soulmate is.

Soul contracts

To fully understand the concept of a soulmate, I think it's helpful to start by exploring the concept of soul contracts. All souls carry a vibrational resonance (that is the after-effect of a vibration) with them through each lifetime. Every experience, lesson and person that soul encounters affects those vibrations, hence any unfinished 'business' from a previous life will carry through to the next as part of that vibrational resonance.

Our intention as a soul, as we progress through various lives, is to grow and expand our consciousness by learning lessons along the way. By acquiring and fulfilling lessons that we have predetermined for ourselves in a soul contract, our souls are able to advance to a higher consciousness.

My introduction to soul contracts came through intuitive psychic, journalist and creator of the *Soul Doctor* podcast Rebecca Dettman. She describes the creation of your soul contract taking place in a big boardroom of sorts up there (author points fervently up at the heavens). When one life ends, before we are able to reincarnate to the next, there is a period of time where we are asked by a higher orchestration to evaluate our previous life—kind of like an end of employment review. What did you learn? What did you feel you could have explored more? What opportunities did you feel you missed out on? What would you like to improve on? Once the previous life has been evaluated, you then have the opportunity to decide what the purpose of your soul will be in the next life. The intention behind a soul contract is to advance your spiritual growth, with the idea that your soul expands with each life it leads.

Perhaps in a past life you had a series of abusive relationships and you were able to learn the lesson of boundaries, so in this lifetime you'd like a breather from trauma and drama. Consequently, you put a harmonious and loving long-term relationship into your soul contract. Perhaps you decide this life is all about loving yourself, so you go through a series of lessons that encourage you to deepen that self-love.

This also means that certain people in your life (especially the ones that deliver an impactful lesson) have been assigned to you *by you* in that big boardroom in the sky. The supporters, the challengers, the lovers, the liars, the narcissistic boss, they were all scheduled in for you by you. I believe Annabel was definitely a soul lesson scheduled into my contract so that I could learn about self-worth, how to treat employees in my own business and the importance of mental health.

When I first heard about the notion of soul contracts, I suddenly felt very powerless. If everything had already been predetermined, did this mean that I had no free will? In short, no. We always have a choice. Think of your soul contract as a blueprint with many paths. You can choose which ones to go down and which to avoid. You might choose to pursue certain paths with enthusiasm and focus, yet wander aimlessly down others time and time again. It might take you several lifetimes to fulfil certain life lessons, and that's okay, too—it is all part of your soul's journey.

Think of it like this: your soul contract is basically a deal that you made with yourself before this life to expand your own consciousness, so any time you choose the path that doesn't encourage growth, and any time you avoid the shadows out of fear even though you know a brighter light waits at the other end, the only person you're cheating is yourself. This premise shifted the entire way I approach life. Any obstacles, heartbreaks and missed opportunities were not a punishment, but an opportunity to step the f*ck up and upgrade my consciousness. This shifted my self-worth monumentally. Suddenly, the things that felt outside of my control were not, because my soul had put them there for my growth. This means that even if you feel like you've gone off course, you never really can—it's all part of your soul's vibrational intent. Comforting, no?

Matt Kahn, author, spiritual teacher and YouTube sensation, says of soul contracts:

> A soul contract usually has a few different premises.
> A contract is either motivating you into an action step
> that is the embodiment of your highest wisdom. [Or]
> you're put into situations that seem unfair [and] unjust
> just to become aware of the judgments you have. And by
> learning to embrace and love the one who judges, that level
> of judgment unravels and you exit that moment more
> evolved than the moment before.

This brings me to soulmates, but we can't discuss the topic of soulmates without also addressing the concept of twin flames. And I think it's so important that you understand the difference between the two, because I bet most of you have confused one for the other for a long time. I know I did.

Twin flames

There are many different interpretations of twin flames out there, but I think the simplest way to describe a twin flame is this: someone who brings the best out of you by guiding you into your wound and shadow work. Their role in your life is to come in like a steam train of emotional turmoil to ultimately guide you back to yourself. Sounds fun, right?

The chemistry with a twin flame is different to other relationships. Here are some ways to identify a twin flame:

★ You feel incredibly aligned and vibrationally matched with this person (and will often confuse them for a soulmate).
★ You're inexplicably drawn to each other, and your two souls feel intertwined.
★ You only need to think about the other person and they call.
★ You can sense their thoughts and feelings without being anywhere near each other.
★ You continually cross paths, even in the most obscure of locations.
★ You know exactly how to push each other's buttons.
★ They sweep in to shake things up whenever they sense you're in a 'good place' and finally have your shit together (this is my favourite twin flame trait). Cheers, mate!

Although having great chemistry with someone who is clearly not good for you feels like a cruel joke, Rebecca Dettman describes this chemistry as the glue that keeps you around long enough to learn the lessons. This is the role of the twin flame: to advance and upgrade your soul. And without the chemistry, well, you wouldn't stick around for that nonsense.

This resonated so much for me when I first heard it. Your 'connection' with your twin flame, and that unexplainable magnetism that keeps them coming in and out of your life right when you think you've got your life as you want it, is necessary for the growth of your soul, otherwise you'd just kick them to the curb.

Beau and I were definitely twin flames. You see our story didn't end after six months of 'I can't do this' and 'I need you'. Oh no, we continued to-ing and fro-ing in various forms for many, many years, much to the confusion of everyone around us. For some of those years, we were happy. We had some blissful and deeply magical moments (this is what formed the glue), but those years were also littered with hellishly dramatic arguments, three-day disappearing acts and bathroom-floor breakdowns (mostly mine). We broke up often, had relationships with other people in between (mostly him) but were drawn back together by our intoxicating and magnetic 'chemistry'. We'd go months, at times years, with zero contact, only to fatefully cross paths in an unexpected place, organise a platonic lunch or dinner, fake a friendship and then find ourselves back in each other's vibrational field, poking and prodding at one another's wounds again. This loop continued for a decade. I slap my forehead just thinking about it.

These twin-flame relationships hold no logic, especially to outsiders who say things like, 'Just leave!' 'She's not good for you.' 'He doesn't make you happy.' 'Why can't you two just forget about each other?' 'You know this never ends well.' But they just don't understand the connection, right?

Back then, a small, naïve and disillusioned part of me thought that all of this back and forth, mind-reading and kismet-type encounters meant Beau and I were eventually destined for each other. But I can say now, without a doubt, that as much as I love, respect and genuinely enjoy Beau's company (even to this day), our entire relationship was a series of soul lessons that both of us were contracted to learn here on earth. Once I was able to go back through and tick each one of them off, our twin-flame soul contract was complete, and that chemistry, that glue, lost its grip.

That relationship taught me lessons aplenty, including what I want and what I don't want in love. What my limits are, what I'm unwilling to compromise on and what I need in a partner. But most importantly, our relationship, in the most roundabout way, brought me back to myself. And that is the role of the twin flame, to bring you back to self—however long and with however much drama it takes.

Of twin flames, Matt Kahn says:

> *The twin flame brings up in you the betrayal,*
> *the disillusionment, the confusion, the heartbreak.*
> *That is the spiritual gift of trying to initiate you*
> *into your highest consciousness by breaking you*
> *completely open if you'll allow it.*

I tell you the story of Beau and I not to air my dirty laundry (or his), but because just about everyone I know has a Beau. Even Beau had a Beau ... it was me (and, controversially, perhaps even the woman before me). And the experience of having a twin flame can feel so deeply personal and at times isolating, but I don't want you to be disillusioned into thinking that the indescribable, unmatchable, I-may-never-experience-this-again chemistry that you have with them means that they are your soulmate or, alternatively, that everything you went through with this person is meaningless. Because all that crap—the back and forth, the drama, the wounding and the intensity—is not a measure of a soulmate, but rather a sign of a twin flame. And you went through all that stuff in order for your soul to grow, upgrade and expand so that eventually you could find your way back to you. And the 'sense of coming home' that people describe when they've found 'the one', it's the feeling of coming home to YOU, my darling, not someone else.

Twin flames catapult you back to self. They are not there to work through the lessons with you, they are there to force you into working out those lessons for yourself. Tough love, but very necessary, and I wouldn't trade a decade of the highs and lows with Beau for anything.

But if we can go back to romanticism and Hollywood for a minute, you'll see how these two things have f*cked up the distinction between twin flame and soulmate big time. May I indulge in a pop-culture reference for one minute?

Sex and the City has a lot to answer for. Big and Carrie Bradshaw were twin flames, not soulmates. #controversial! They treated each other like shit for six+ years, swanning in and out of each other's lives, especially when one of them was seemingly doing well, but they were powerless to avoid the chemistry (or glue). Big's purpose was not to be Carrie's Prince Charming, but to force her to grow and learn about her own self-worth. And although I never wanted Carrie to end up with that Russian douchebag at the end of the series, she should never have ended up with Big either. When the writers came up with that plotline, they convinced every single girl in the world that if you wait around long enough and put up with enough crap then he will eventually realise that you're meant to be!

Puh-lease! #TeamAiden all the way!

Soulmates

Unlike a twin flame, a soulmate will remind you of your worth and keep you accountable to your light. There is still an incredible vibrational alignment and chemistry, but it's easy, effortless, balanced and comforting. Your soulmate will reflect lessons back to you for you to grow and upgrade, but you're able to work on them together as a team.

A true soulmate connection allows both parties to be heard, understood and respected, and arguments and disagreements work themselves out naturally, and without the drama and intensity that comes with other less-kismet unions.

I have two very strong beliefs about soulmates that I'd like to share with you. The first is this: I believe we encounter a romantic soulmate when we have cleaned up our act and found completeness within ourselves.

There is a massive misunderstanding that finding your soulmate will complete you, and that any gaps in your life will be filled by them. There's this false notion that once you unite, all of your faults will be fixed, all of your questions will be answered and all of your insecurities will disappear. That is just not true.

You are a whole human being. There is no 'lost' part of you aimlessly walking around, waiting to be found in the aisles of second-hand bookshops or in hipster bars. Your search for your other half is futile; all you are searching for is your own completeness (see Chapter 9 if you need reminding of this). Soulmate connections are the pairing of two complete souls. The gaps you think a partner will fill, the missing pieces you're longing to connect with, can only be filled by you. And your soulmate is on the same journey. They, too, are arriving as a whole; they're not looking for you to fix them, change them or fill a void. You have come together to complement each other and grow, expand and upgrade as a unit.

My second belief (brace yourself!) is that I don't believe in 'the one' (GASP!). I believe that we can have more than one soulmate in a lifetime. Many people (mostly on the internet) will disagree with me on this, and everyone is entitled to their own opinion, but I truly believe that sometimes a fully aligned, enchanted and highly vibrational match can come into our lives for a certain period of time and then leave ... and that's okay.

I also don't believe that on this large, expansive planet called Earth there are a designated handful of souls that we're destined to meet. Just imagine! You'd have to cross your fingers and all of your toes that your paths crossed, and that you weren't looking down at the pavement (or your iPhone) when they did. I believe there is an infinite collection of vibrational matches in this world for everyone, and as you go through life your vibrations shift and will align with other souls, and then they'll shift again to welcome new souls into your orbit. Your only job is to worry about radiating authenticity, and your vibrations will ensure you end up in the same room as people on your frequency.

UPPING THOSE GOOD LOVE VIBES

So how do we increase our love vibrations? First, let's get clear on what kind of a vibration love is. It's true that love is complicated, but love, at its essence, is also a really simple feeling. Romanticism and pop culture urge us to layer it in sexual intensity, dramatic plotlines, emotional despair and the pressure of finding a love that transcends time and space, but that's a reputation that love never asked for. Love is not an attainable force, it is not something that you find, love is something that *you are* and have always been.

The language that we attach to love is also incredibly misleading. Having a 'crush' on someone, being 'crazy' in love, 'madly' in love, 'falling' in love. ALL of the drama and none of the true essence of love! For so long, when trying to manifest more love in my life, I would tap into the vibrations of how I had experienced love in the past. But love for me had

Exercise 25
A CONVERSATION WITH LOVE

This is another free-writing exercise, so grab your journal and a pen. Have a conversation with Love. Ask it all of the questions that puzzle you or render you incapable of fully embracing it in each and every moment. Talk to Love about your fears and wait for the responses.

As you write, don't pause or edit, just let the stream of consciousness between you and Love flood freely out and onto the page until there is nothing left. Trust me when I say this exercise is transformational.

always been messy, intense and dramatic; those experiences were not shining examples of love, and I didn't want to create more of that in my life. So when I tapped into what I thought was the vibration of love, what I was actually doing was tapping into fear, insecurity and past stories of love.

Early on in this book, I suggested tapping into the vibration of love by watching a cheesy rom-com that makes you love love. But now that you're better versed in the ins and outs of manifestation, this advice comes with a caveat: can you tap into the feelings without attaching to the story? Can you have a remembrance of the sensations you felt when Harry and Sally finally got together, without attaching the story and years of mess (and plotlines) that got them to that point? Because, as I've been saying throughout this chapter, those stories are for entertainment, yet we subconsciously model how we're meant to feel in love on them. And we gotta stop!

Love is not a story or a series of obstacles, it is a pure essence and vibration that has been instilled in you since the point of your conception (perhaps even earlier). Love is where you come from, it's what you're made of and it's the secret ingredient behind manifesting your future.

My friend, soul sister, kinesiologist and mentor Zoe Bosco of Medicinal Alchemy, set me a beautiful exercise when I sat down to write this chapter. I was becoming so consumed by my past stories around love that I became completely paralysed over the message of this chapter, which is getting to the pure essence of love. Zoe asked me a simple question, 'What is love to you?' I had no response. I thought about it, I tried to feel into it ... but nothing. 'I don't bloody know!' I thought, the weight of that simple question rendering me speechless. 'Well, why don't you ask Love?' (Long silence) 'I want you to have a conversation with Love. I want you to ask Love all of the questions you need answers to. I then want you to reply as Love. You know the answers.' She was right. I did.

Here's a snapshot of my own conversation with Love:

> **Me:** *Hey, Love. How do you feel?*
>
> **Love:** *Right now I feel detached from you—like you're scared to really feel me. Is that true?*
>
> **Me:** *Yes. That is true. You have set me up for so much pain in the past, I think I'm scared to feel you too deeply in case I get swept back into the same heartache and despair.*
>
> **Love:** *I'm not here to plummet you into darkness, my darling, I'm here to show you the light. All you need to do is have faith in yourself and believe in my ability to heal. That's it. Every heartache you*

experienced while feeling me was for your growth, not your demise. It was to show you the possibilities of what you're capable of and what you can overcome, and how, through the contraction of pain, an expansive and upgraded you was able to emerge. Jord, you have shown up for every challenge put in your path by having the intuitive knowing that the solution to heartache is to love yourself more. Only from this space can you attempt to love others and allow them to love you. You've shown bravery, courage, resilience and, above all else, grace. And because of this, you've uncovered the secret that everyone is eternally searching for: You ARE love.

He is coming. He has always been coming, you just needed to clear and overcome lessons so that he didn't become collateral damage. He has been doing the same. When you two finally unite, it will be to grow together through love and with love, not to use love as a dagger or a shield.

Me: How much longer will I need to wait? I am grateful for the lessons and I know my time is coming, but, LIKE, WHEN?

Love: It is already here, Jord. It has been happening behind the scenes for many moons. This book is one of the final pieces. The theme of this book is self-worth, and you needed to fully embody it, write about it and then share it for all of the pieces to fall into place. Your deep love for self is what makes this book possible, and that's what will bring him in, Jord. You know that better than anyone else.

This book is your learnings. It is your call to arms. You know it and I know it. The universe knows it. He knows it. Don't let that scare you or paralyse you, let it lift you to great heights. You've got this! I love you. I just need you to keep on loving yourself, always.

Me: Cheers, Love. Good chat. x

So, if love is our essence, and the only way to feel it more is to love ourselves more deeply, then it's fair to say that you can't really lose love, fall out of love, own love or give love away. All you can do is BE love, embody love, express love and have faith that the vibrational frequency of love will gain strength, radiate and attract more love towards you in each and every moment.

MANIFESTING LOVE WITH THE MANIFESTATION EQUATION

Okay, so now that you have a better understanding of how love has been misinterpreted through the different filters we've placed on it (i.e. Romanticism, the Hollywood effect, language and our own stories), it's time to get down to business.

But before we get started, I just want to be clear that manifesting love doesn't require you to be single. Perhaps you want to manifest more love in an existing relationship. Perhaps you're not even interested in manifesting romantic love; perhaps your goal is to manifest more love within your extended family, through your friendships, or even to uncover a passion for the work you do. Whatever type of love you seek, know that the only thing you require to get started is an understanding that you already ARE love.

Thoughts

We've all got a bunch of stories about love, and I've already told you a few of mine. If the stories of my exes were episodes of *Friends*, they'd be 'The One with the High School Sweetheart', 'The One with the Prostitutes',

Exercise 26
IDENTIFYING YOUR LOVE STORIES

In the money chapter, we rewrote our money story. If you feel called to, you can do the same with your love story, but for the purposes of this exercise I merely want you to identify what stories you continue to tell when it comes to your love life.

Perhaps you tell stories about how you were mistreated or how you messed up something great. Maybe your story is about the one that got away, or your terrible track record. Whatever your story is, just grab your journal and write it down.

'The One with the Twin Flame', 'The One with the Drinking Problem', 'The One with the Anger Issues' and 'The One who was Perfectly Unattainable'. None of these were actually 'The One'.

As much as I like to use these stories for comic relief as well as reasons for why I haven't settled down as I approach my mid-thirties, the truth is telling these stories—either out loud or to myself—keeps the energy around them active. They become more than just stories; they become part of my energetic make-up and the frequency of my vibrations around love.

Here are a few other stories I used to love spreading like wildfire in order to justify why I was still single: it is so hard to meet men in Sydney. There are no decent conscious men out there. All the good men are taken or gay. I'm too busy concentrating on work right now to fall in love.

Once we can identify our stories, we can see them for what they are: just stories! They are not your truth, and they are not worthy of affecting your energy around love. Now that you know exactly what they are, you're going to let them go, got it? Because the more you indulge in your past, the further away you get from enjoying the present and manifesting a worthy future.

Stories become the framework for the limiting beliefs we set up around why we haven't found the one or why we're incapable of loving, or whatever your belief is around why you're not experiencing love.

Here's a taste of the limiting beliefs I formed through the stories I told about my relationship history: I attract losers. I'm unlucky in love. I'm not attractive, skinny, smart, tall or funny enough ... Actually that last one's not true—I'm very funny. But you get the gist.

Many (read: all) of your limiting beliefs around love have nothing to do with the other person and everything to do with what you believe about your own worth. One of my limiting beliefs around love was that no guy would ever be proud to show me off as his girlfriend. Sure, I'd make his mates laugh at parties, but a part of me felt badly for him that he ended up with a girlfriend who had cellulite on her butt and less-than-perfect breasts.

I uncovered that limiting belief by doing Exercise 26, and honestly I was shocked. I didn't even realise that I was running that subconscious thought on an endless, self-deprecating loop. If limiting beliefs around your self-worth come up, I encourage you to go back to Chapter 9, because it all starts with self-love, my friend.

Feelings

I recall getting into a fiery discussion with an ex (it's irrelevant which 'the one' he was) about the way he was making me feel. Here I was trying to express my feelings with clear and open communication, and all he could say to me in return was, 'I can't MAKE you feel anything, only you can

Exercise 27

GIFT YOURSELF A GOLDEN LOVE NUGGET

Why is it that we always have plenty of advice for friends about love, but we can never view our own situation in the same objective light? As I'm dishing out golden nuggets to friends, I often think, 'Wow, this is good! I should really follow my own advice.'

It's time to be your own best friend! Start by asking yourself questions that will uncover the limiting beliefs you hold around love. Get the ball rolling by answering these questions:

☾ Why am I not in a relationship?

☾ Why am I still in this relationship?

☾ What am I afraid of?

☾ What is stopping me from feeling love right now in this very moment?

☾ What is the recurring pattern in my love life?

☾ What does love feel like?

Answer those questions and any more you can come up with as honestly as possible. Then I want you to give advice to yourself as an impartial observer of your situation rather than the participant. If your best friend voiced their limiting beliefs around their own relationship potential, what advice would you give them?

control how you're feeling.' Ooh! This aggravated me beyond belief because he was making me feel so angry, so frustrated and so f*cking helpless, but he was also right … Dammit!

Nobody can *make* you feel anything. You hold all of the power when it comes to your feelings. And although people can act in a way that may trigger you to feel a certain emotion, you always have the choice to stay in it or choose a more helpful and useful vibration.

I raise this now because relationships are a wonderful trigger for this kind of mentality when it comes to how we're feeling. When you're in a partnership with someone else, it can be easy to become consumed by their feelings and vice versa, to the point that it becomes tricky to distinguish between your feelings and theirs. But no matter how incredibly connected you are to someone, you are always responsible for your own feelings. You hear me?

If ever you find yourself relinquishing responsibility for your own feelings due to someone else's words or actions, take the power back with a few deep breaths. Know that feeling hurt, angry, upset or frustrated is a reflection of your feelings about *your* own self-worth and that those words or actions have been triggered by their feelings about *their* own self-worth. If I've learned anything about passionate arguments where accusations start flying and feelings get trampled on, it's that taking a 'time out' so each party can evaluate their own reactions and the true meaning behind them is essential. It's the only way to get out alive.

HOW DO YOU WANT LOVE TO FEEL?

Uncovering your past stories and limiting beliefs around love is sure to dredge up some old feelings around how you feel in, around and out of love. But if you were to just BE love and choose love in each and every moment, what other feelings would bloom?

When it comes to manifesting love, many of the teachings suggest writing down the traits of your ideal partner. I have to say I am not a fan of this tactic for a couple of reasons. First, it sets up a bunch of boundaries and parameters around what your ideal partner should be. Are you sure he or she needs to be a suit with a high-flying job? Is it really that important that they come from a large family? Not only will specifics like these limit you, but what if a person possessing the combination of all of those qualities doesn't exist? Honestly, I think it's a manifestation nightmare, plus we already know the universe loves sending unexpected surprises!

Secondly, when we write a list like this, it's almost as if the list itself takes on its own vibration, and what happens then is that the list, rather than you, starts vibrating on the same frequency as the other person. If you're keen to write a list, focus instead on how you want to *feel* in your ideal relationship.

If love were a plant that grew when watered with self-love and limitless beliefs about your own self-worth, and it bloomed with other supportive and love-fuelled feelings, what would you desire those feelings to be?

ALL OF THE FEELS!

The deeper you dive into the practice of manifestation, the sooner you'll uncover common vibrational themes across many aspects of your life. For example, I want to feel freedom, abundance and peace in my romantic relationships, but also in my finances, at work *and* when it comes to my own self-worth. And whether you make the decision consciously or not, once you begin manifesting a certain feeling in one area, the ripple effect is that you'll experience an overarching sense of that feeling in everything that you do.

So with this in mind, let's work backwards. You now know how you want to feel in a relationship, and by tapping into those feelings you will

Exercise 28
LOVE-FUELLED FEELINGS

Write a comprehensive list of all the feelings you want to feel in a loving relationship. Not how you want a partner to *make* you feel, but rather the feelings that will form your love vibration.

To clarify, you're not writing down physical or material traits, but rather how YOU want to feel when you're with that person. It is that vibration that will attract a partner with a similar vibration to you, regardless of whether they wear a suit or a turtleneck and Timberlands.

If you're already in a relationship, this exercise will totally work for you, too. How do you want to feel in your current relationship? What feelings are you currently missing out on?

Use this exercise to gain clarity around how you're currently feeling and how you desire to feel.

attract a partner with a similar vibration. What would happen if you also cultivated those feelings in other areas of your life where you find accessing peace, abundance and excitement a little more effortless?

When do you feel truly free? What activity cultivates a sense of peace deep inside you? In what part of your life do you feel an overflowing abundance? The intention is to start shifting all of your vibrations to be completely aligned with the feelings you want to generate around a relationship so that those very same vibrations are magnetised to you (hopefully in the form of your perfect match).

To my coupled up friends, I want you to undergo the same exploration with your feelings, but I also want you to sit down with your partner and communicate with them. I know, it's novel and innovative to talk to them, but it works! If this feels strange at first, just take small steps. Talk to them about how you're feeling right now, and what you desire to be feeling in your relationship. Be mindful not to put blame on them for not *making* you feel a certain way, but instead focus on letting them know that you're struggling to feel the way you'd like to. Having these honest conversations will mean you can work together and can workshop ways that you can both start feeling more of what you want to and less of what you don't. It's important to ask them to share their feelings, too. Perhaps you're both longing to feel the same thing and don't even know it.

You could try saying something along these lines:

> *I'd like to feel more connection in our relationship.*
> *How would you feel about prioritising dinner together*
> *once a week?*

> *I want to feel more supported in our relationship.*
> *When I can express myself and feel heard without*
> *judgment, I feel supported. Are you able to listen*
> *when I share my challenges with you?*

Once you've shared with each other, it's time for you to start working on vibrating those feelings as much as possible. When you're in a relationship with someone you love and you start vibrating joy or peace, it often shifts their vibration almost instantly. We may say we want more support, connection or romance, but have we been giving it?

Actions

I'm going to gift you some super-practical action steps to manifest new love and reignite existing love, but let's start by actively increasing our overall love vibration from the inside out with these simple action steps:

LOVE THYSELF

I've been harping on about this through the entire book, and there's plenty more of it to come. There's no avoiding it, my friend: until you can accept and love yourself fully, you'll never feel adequately loved by another. Self-love is not about self-improvement, it's about self-acceptance. The minute you accept yourself for who you are right now in this very moment, your authenticity will attract your perfect vibrational match.

LOVE AND LIGHT

Whenever I find it tricky to access the vibration of love, I start super teeny tiny and go from there. Do this with me now using this simple visualisation exercise.

> *Close your eyes and bring your awareness to a tiny pinprick of white light in the centre of your heart space. This is the essence of love deep inside of you. With each inhale breath, feel that white light grow ever so slightly, and with each exhale feel it infuse your cells with the vibration of love. Continue this exercise, visualising the white light expanding with each breath, until your entire body is radiating with the vibration of love. As you go about your day, send beams of this white light out into the world. Smile at strangers and see the transference of love and light from your smile to theirs. Send that light to everyone you encounter, whether it's in person, via email or across social media.*

Have you heard the expression 'love is infectious'? Well, it's true, most feelings are. Radiate love as often as possible, and watch it catch like wildfire.

DO MORE OF WHAT YOU LOVE

What are your passions? What do you love doing? Are there activities, experiences or other people that just kick up your love barometer? Get more of those things in your life! It sounds so simple, but we often prioritise what we think we should be doing (e.g. drinking green smoothies, body brushing and getting a good night's sleep) over a fun weekend away with best friends, enjoying a decadent eighteen-course degustation dinner with matching wines or watching reruns of *Gilmore Girls* with a packet of corn chips and some homemade guac. #guilty #loveit! I'm not encouraging couch potato-itis (it's a thing) over green vegetables, I'm simply saying that doing what you love and allowing love to vibrate through your cells can be much healthier than following a click-bait listicle of self-love practices.

BEAUTY IS IN THE EYE OF THE ONE
WITH THE HIGH-LOVE VIBES

Beauty is all around us, and I'm not talking about Victoria's Secret models or fitspo influencers, I'm talking about sunrises, waterfalls, jacaranda trees, random acts of kindness, puppies, laughing children and the smell of jasmine in spring. It's everywhere, and all you have to do is open your senses to experience it. Observing beauty in even the tiniest things places a positive filter on all of your encounters, increasing your high vibrations. The more you allow yourself to feel love for the world around you, the easier it is to identify love within yourself.

WHY YOU'RE STILL SINGLE

Now that we know how to cultivate the love that is within us and be a living and breathing embodiment of love, it's time to strut those love vibes around town and attract an equally high-vibing partner. But here's the thing: I have a string of beautiful, successful, funny, smart and sexy girlfriends who are very single. And I say 'very' to let you know that it hasn't just been a couple of weeks or months between dates, but years. And while everyone has a personal story (or stories) to explain why they're still kicking it solo, we all have a few things in common. So let's take a time-out to explore the single gal's (and the bachelor's) paradox.

We profess it's really hard to meet decent men/women, yet we don't leave the house. What are we waiting for? Is our future partner going to walk through our front door unexpectedly? (This actually did happen to me with one of 'the ones', but that was an exception, not a rule ... and here I am and there he is). I confess that Romanticism sometimes rules my rationale around this. A spontaneous, fate-driven moment that is meant to be, perhaps on the pedestrian crossing of a busy New York street (even though I live in Sydney and haven't been to New York in years), a casual sideways glance at a general store in a small coastal town we're both passing through on our way to the same wedding, riding my bike through the rice fields of Ubud only to be knocked off by a handsome Brazilian in his Jeep. (Oh wait, that's Liz Gilbert's story in Eat Pray Love! My bad.) But you get it. Our fantasies keep us safe, and although I'm an out and proud introvert who really values a Friday night at home, the truth is that the reason I'm probably not meeting men is because it is literally impossible to run into them in the lounge room of my own apartment.

We dismiss advances. Do you know how many times I've turned to a single girlfriend and said, 'Excuse me, he is totally flirting with you,' and she's replied, 'Oh no, he's just being friendly.' Or how about all those strangers in the street that you completely miss engaging with because you avoid eye contact, or all of the potential partners that you swipe left on when scrolling through dating apps, even though they've boldly swiped right for you. If you're not open to receiving advances, you're not going to see them, even when they're blindingly obvious to everyone else around you. Time to pick up on those signals!

We are super picky about things that don't matter. I have a girlfriend I love to death and she's going to cringe when she reads this, but she cannot get past grey hair in men under fifty. So much so that she would happily dismiss a kind, generous, funny and loving man if he was prematurely grey. I have another friend who will cease contact with a guy if she finds out that he googled her, and another friend who will not date men who wear glasses because of a spectacle-sporting ex who ruined things for every other sight-impaired man out there. It sounds ridiculous, but many of us have similar hang-ups. This is why I ask you to abandon the physical and material traits listed under 'deal-breakers' in your mind and instead focus on how you want to *feel* with a potential partner. Think about all of those wonderful, conscious and intelligent men out there who prefer not to wear contact lenses that you could be passing by.

They can take our (single) lives, but they'll never take our freedom! There are a trillion positives that come out of spending lengthy periods of time uncoupled, but the greatest gift I believe you gain from the single life is your independence. And nothing hones, refines and strengthens it more than a little solo time. The thing is, once you finally nail the whole independent woman thang, you're terrified of letting it go. Once the chemistry (and hormones) kick in during the first stages of dating, we worry that our independence will be the first thing to be compromised. And this isn't just a Destiny's Child all-the-women-who-are-independent-type deal, men aren't immune to this fear of loss of freedom. But I've got good news: you can keep your independence *and* be in a relationship!

I make all of these points, not to rat my single friends out, but merely to point out that not only are many of us 'singles' not actively looking for a partner (even though we really want one), we're also actively *avoiding* relationships without even realising it.

Which brings me to some really practical action steps that you can start taking TODAY to manifest a relationship.

THE NO-EXCUSES ACTION PLAN

We're about three-quarters into this book, so I feel like we know each other pretty well now. I'm going to hedge my bets and say you're going to read this list, and be like, 'Yeah, I know this stuff.' And I get it, I'm sure you do know this stuff. But how much of it are you actually practising and putting into action? So instead of rolling your eyes at the simplicity of these action steps, I want you to make a promise to this book and to yourself that you will implement at least one of these practical steps this week, if not today! Also, banish any childhood program you're still running around stranger danger. A stranger is just a friend or potential soulmate you haven't met yet! Okay, we good?

1. **Smile at strangers in the street, and hold eye contact while they smile back.** Sounds simple enough, but out of fear of rejection many of us won't wait to receive a smile in return. And you know

what, you might not get a smile back, but if you don't that's okay. You'll survive, I promise. If someone doesn't smile back, it says absolutely nothing about you; it says way more about them.

2. **Start a conversation with a stranger.** This is my mother's superpower, and although it embarrassed me greatly as a kid, I admire it now. The stranger doesn't have to be a potential partner, but by exchanging vibrations with them you're automatically widening your vibrational field, and you never know what that might lead to.

3. **Put yourself on a dating app.** Okay, before you give me a flat-out no, listen up! I haven't had much success with dating apps myself, but my friends have. And what I do enjoy about them is how easy it is to set up an actual real-life date. Walking into a bar, chatting up a potential suitor, slipping them your number and hoping they'll call is way harder than swiping right, chatting for a bit to make sure they're not crazy and then arranging a time to meet for a drink (plus you can do it while chilling on the couch #win). But in order for this to work, I have a little challenge for you.

   ★ Join a dating app if you're not on one already.
   ★ Set up a profile that is 100 per cent authentic to you. Don't say you like sports if you don't. Don't put up photos from five years ago. You're trying to attract a match for the person you are, not who you think they want.
   ★ For every three guys or gals you swipe right for (that means you're interested), I want you to also swipe right for someone who you wouldn't usually go for. Maybe not the guy pictured

with the beer bong or the chick with the collection of taxidermy (each to their own), but someone you'd usually be quick to dismiss. I once matched with a guy who I never bothered messaging because I was a bit like 'meh', but he ended up tracking me down through social media (in a non-creepy way) and we went out on a bunch of really lovely dates, so you just never know.

4. **Accept compliments and give them in return.** I suggested this one in the self-worth chapter, and it absolutely applies here, too. We're so quick to dismiss people's interest in us, but an acceptance of self allows an expectation for people to be interested in us. And that doesn't make you arrogant, it just means you think you're wonderful and it's not a surprise that other people do, too.

5. **If you've always done something one way, try doing it a different way this time.** Radical, I know, but it's very easy to get stuck in the same monotonous traps. If you always date the same type of guy or gal, hang out at all the same bars and go to all the same barbecues with the same coupled-up friends, then it's time to try something new. You've already joined a dating app (right?), so why not sign up for French lessons, or go out with that guy your friend at work wants to set you up with, or simply go to a bar in a different suburb. This stuff doesn't have to be revolutionary, just different.

6. **Shake up the energy around you.** I lived in the same apartment from the ages of twenty-one to thirty-four. That's thirteen years! That apartment witnessed five of 'the ones', one of whom lived there with me for a period of time. There was so much old energy

flying around that apartment from the ghosts of boyfriends past that it really didn't matter how much I saged it, the energy was keeping me stuck. I stayed for so long because among the chaos that is adult life, that apartment was my one constant and it supported me well. But that's a very long time to be stewing in the energy of your formative years, so just as I was wrapping up writing this book, I packed up my little apartment and, in doing so, left my ghosts behind me. Stay tuned ...

7. **Take note of your relationship patterns.** Are you attracting the same people over and over again? What is the lesson here? Relationships are almost always a mirror of how we feel about ourselves and what we need to address within ourselves. What are your past relationships showing you that you need to address in yourself?

Faith

The best relationship advice I've ever been given was from 'the One who was Perfectly Unattainable'. He travelled for work. Well, he worked in Hong Kong and would travel back to Sydney to see me. And although he promised he was always coming back, I couldn't handle the uncertainty. He would say, 'Jord, can you just try to stay in the present with me? You spend half your time reminding me of things that happened in the past and the other half worrying about the future. Can't you just enjoy right now with me?' In the moment it's hard to hear such freaking clarity, but he was so right.

Because you are now well versed on how vibrations work, you'll understand that when we hang out in our past stories and bring them into the present moment by judging, comparing or obsessing about them, we're also inviting the energy of the past to take up residence in the present moment. By doing this, we continue to manifest the same vibrations again and again. And equally, if you spend your energy future projecting, stressing and worrying about situations that haven't happened yet, you're creating vibrations that will ultimately manifest that reality.

None of this is helpful in dating or relationships. In fact, it's what kills most healthy relationships and blocks potential relationships from eventuating. The only thing I've found to help me stay present in these moments is to practise faith. How to practise having faith in this situation differs slightly from other chapters because not only do you need to have faith in yourself and the universe, but you also have to have complete faith in a whole other human being—one with their own set of limiting beliefs, stories and future projections. If you can practise having faith in yourself, the universe and the other person, you'll have no desire to be anywhere other than there with them in the present moment. This doesn't mean that you can't discuss and plan your future with your partner, it just means being conscious of creating low vibrations through negative expectations or future predictions and, in turn, subconsciously manifesting them.

TRUST THE TIMING OF YOUR LIFE

In 1966, The Supremes sang, 'You can't hurry love, no you just have to wait', and ain't that the truth! I have come leaps and bounds in my love life in the past three years. I have learned a bunch of lessons and implemented the learnings from them. I am constantly nurturing my self-worth through practising self-acceptance and using my intuition. I smile at strangers. I actively date. I sprinkle love and light all over

Exercise 29
THE TREE OF LOVE

Your final exercise for this chapter is a little creative project that I've adapted over the years. I often use this in my workshops to get people out of their heads.

You'll need colourful pens or pencils AND a large piece of paper (I like using butcher's paper because then my tree can be as tall as I like).

Step 1: Draw the outline of a large tree. It must include roots, a thick trunk and branches.

Step 2: The roots of the tree represent your new beliefs about love. Write them as positive and present intentions. For example, I am love. I am at peace with love. I trust in commitment and connection. I effortlessly attract conscious and available men/women. Love is abundant in my life.

Step 3: The trunk of the tree represents the feelings you want to vibrate in love and relationships. These might be peace, freedom, abundance, security, stability and excitement.

Step 4: The branches of the tree are the actions that support your intentions. Write your action steps along the branches. For example, I open my eyes and my heart to new possibilities. I smile and make eye contact with strangers. I receive compliments from people without deflecting them. I show up for love. I radiate love out into the world.

Step 5: Finally, add some leaves to your tree. These are your love adornments. They are the things that make you feel the high vibrations of love—activities you absolutely love doing, such as writing, practising yoga, spending time with a pet, reading in bed on a Sunday morning, volunteering, meditating.

Place your Tree of Love somewhere that you will see it every day, as a reminder to tap into the vibrations of love and take action steps in the direction of love.

the place like confetti. I am open, willing and goddamn ready ... yet I'm still single.

This used to drive me Gwen Stefani-style B-A-N-A-N-A-S. I'd slowly slip into a self-worth spiral of I'm not enough, he's not out there and what's wrong with me ... but you know what? I can, without a doubt, say that the only reason I am still single and haven't met someone that I want to share my completeness and love vibrations with is because it just isn't time.

And I know, it sounds like something only single people say, but it is the truth. There are so many things I've had to do first. I had to sort through those twin-flame soul lessons so I didn't have any more unfinished business; I had to find space to progress in my career the way I wanted to; I had to climb metaphorical mountains and have experiences independently; I also had to write a life-changing book (that's this one, in case that wasn't clear). I'm certain I wouldn't have been able to do any of these things had I been in a relationship. And that's not to say you can't do great things while in a relationship, because you can, but I know that my soul needed to experience the magic that comes from being alone.

We touched on trusting in the timing of your life in Chapter 2, and now that you know all about soul contracts, perhaps my point of view makes a little more sense. When you're seemingly doing everything 'right', and things don't seem to be manifesting as you'd like, having faith that your soul decided that this was the best path for you in this lifetime can be surprisingly reassuring.

If I get super real with myself and dive deep into my inner knowing and intuition, it's saying 'Jordanna Levin, you are in the process of creating a completeness that will bring you the kind of love worth waiting for.'

Because the last thing you want is to meet the perfect and complete soul while you're still sorting through your own soul lessons and limiting beliefs. Trust that when you do the work and the universe deems it to be the right time, then the essence of love that is already inside of you will attract the perfect soul connection. Not before, not never, not too late, but at exactly the right time.

Whenever you feel disconnected from love, remember that every cell in your body is radiating with the essence of love. Every action you take, every word you utter, every thought or feeling you have and every choice you make is the essence of love. You can't fall in or out of love, you can't ever be without love and you can't ever lose love because love is inside of you, it is part of you. You are love.

So go on then, go be love.

CHAPTER 12

Manifesting Your Dream Career

Good news: this chapter is going to appeal to you whether you're ready to walk out of your current job or hoping to improve your current work situation. Perhaps you're trying to figure out your next career move or getting ready to start a new business. Whatever your situation, there are some true gems coming up—so let's get into it.

I have already spoken a bit about my career in this book—the epic highs and the catastrophic lows. And when I look back at my work history, I can see that the superpower I possess when it comes to my career (no matter which hat I happen to be wearing) is the ability to recognise a toxic situation and pivot to a more energetically rewarding experience.

I have already told you that I've manifested dream job after dream job, but what I haven't mentioned is the fact that I have (to varying degrees) reinvented myself professionally over ten times in twelve years. I've been a journalist, marketing assistant, food writer, chef, editor, recipe developer, health coach, yoga teacher, meditation facilitator, retreat caterer, manifestation mentor and now I'm a published author. Some might categorise me as flighty or say I can't settle down, but the truth is I have loved and felt aligned with each and every one of those roles, right up until the time that I didn't. And when that moment came, I pivoted. And in doing so, I found one incredible opportunity after the next.

Many people label me as lucky, but I know that the real reason doors always open for me is because I'm not afraid to close a door that isn't allowing me to vibrate as the best version of me. When I was working for Annabel in my 'dream job', the pivot point presented itself to me as clear as day. We'd just wrapped up a team meeting during which Annabel had ripped me to shreds in front of my peers and junior staff members. This was not a rare occurrence; in fact, it had become the norm.

Walking out of that meeting, a junior member of the team came running up to me and said, 'Are you okay? I can't believe you're not crying. She was so horrible to you. Why are you not upset?' She wasn't wrong. Annabel *had* been horrible to me. So why wasn't I upset? Annabel constantly stuck her claws into me over nothing, but my skin had grown so thick that her behaviour no longer penetrated the surface—I'd become immune to her attacks and numb to my own feelings. I had switched off all emotions and was in full shutdown and protection mode. And I didn't like that person. Sure, I was proud to be strong enough not to take every little criticism personally in the workplace, but I certainly didn't want to be the person who couldn't feel anything when she was being bullied. By allowing this to continue, I was far from being in alignment with who I truly was and I wasn't sure I'd be able to find my way back, so I resigned. The very next day, I received two incredible job opportunities. I accepted both of them.

Once I left that job, I prioritised my own self-worth over any dream-job status. Never again did I compromise my own mental and physical health for the progression of someone else's fame and fortune. If I felt my own authenticity being compromised (as it often can be when you work for high-profile types), I would reassess the situation. Sometimes it was a simple shuffle of my own energy output; sometimes it was an immediate extraction. But I never felt as though I was doing myself a disservice by not sticking with it, settling for mediocre or prioritising other interests over my own intuition.

DO YOU ENJOY BEING AT WORK?

If you want to quit your job, I'll be the first to help you do it. We spend so many of our waking hours at work, and it is such a waste to be using that energy for low vibrations like dread, fear and high anxiety. You want to be able to get to work and say, 'I love rocking up to work each day, and I'm proud of the high vibrations I have when I am here.' The good news is that improving your work situation doesn't mean you have to resign. Sometimes, the situation just requires a few tweaks, and energy just needs to be redirected in a more useful way.

We all have very different work situations, but I want to make one thing very clear: Your purpose, your truth, your calling, your passion (or whatever you want to call it) doesn't necessarily have to be part of your working life. Working in a job that *doesn't* fulfil your purpose here on earth doesn't automatically make it unsuitable for you. Controversially, I encourage clients to reconsider turning their passion into their career *unless* they're willing to feel a full spectrum of feelings around that passion. You don't want to merely survive at work, you want to thrive, and it is absolutely not mandatory to turn your purpose into your career in order to feel this.

I'm sure you've heard people say, 'Do what you love, and you'll never work a day in your life.' Well, I just don't agree with that. If anything, you'll work harder and be tested even more than in any other job. All of this isn't to say you shouldn't work in a field you enjoy or that your business can't reflect your passion, it's merely to caution you and encourage you to be aware that putting pressure on your passion can come with its own set of hardships.

For example, I've always loved food and cooking, which is why I spent eight years in the food publishing industry. But when I created my own business entirely around food, it put a tonne of pressure on this passion, and cooking became a bit of chore. Suddenly, all of my energy was going into writing and developing recipes for clients, preparing food for catering jobs and curating food shots for my social media. I stopped enjoying the art of preparing food for myself. In fact, I stopped cooking for myself completely, unless peanut butter on toast still counts as cooking (it doesn't). The dinner parties I once threw for friends on a regular basis ceased because the last thing I felt like doing after a week of cooking was more cooking. The food styling I'd once loved and prided myself on suddenly held no appeal for me. I even found myself losing interest in dining out and trying new restaurants because food just didn't excite me the way it used to.

The thing I took the most pride in when it came to my business was the love and positive energy that I put into food creation. But when I made food creation the sole focus of my career and the means by which I made my living day in and day out, that positive energy began to drain away. Eventually, all I was putting into food creation was resentment and exhaustion. Slowly, those low vibrations started to affect the success of my business.

APPLYING THE MANIFESTATION EQUATION TO YOUR CAREER

If you can't say that you love rocking up to your work each day, then it's time to unpack your current work situation using the Manifestation Equation, because as wonderful as the equation is for manifesting your dream job, it's also a great tool for helping you to understand how you manifested your current situation.

Exercise 30
UNPACKING YOUR CURRENT WORK SITUATION

Grab your journal and a pen, and ask yourself the following questions. Is there anything about your current work situation that you are dissatisfied with? If so, what is it? The content? The role? Specific people? Your boss? The hours? The environment? The commute?

Write down everything about your job that isn't working for you.

Once you're clear about what is making your job an unhappy situation, ask yourself the following questions.

☾ Is any of this stuff preventable or changeable?

☾ Is it worth the energy of trying to make improvements, or is it time to go? (Be honest! Intuitively, you already know the answer.)

When I was working for Annabel, I would ask anyone who would listen if I should leave my job. Most answered with, 'You'd be crazy, it's a dream role.' Even my close friends and family thought I was being overly dramatic when I threatened to resign. 'What are you going to do if you leave?' they'd say. 'Just try not to engage with her, and you'll be fine.' But when that pivotal moment presented itself, I knew in my heart that I was past the point of ignoring her. By that time, the toxicity in my work life had leached into the rest of my life. When you know you know, and now that you're familiar with how opportunities manifest, you'll know that closing one door means another is sure to open. Check in with yourself to find answers; don't search for them externally.

In order for new doors to start opening, you need to be clear on what the alternative to your current situation would look like.

Thoughts

I bet you could give hundreds of excuses for why you can't possibly leave your job or why you choose to stay in your current unsatisfactory situation. Believe me, I've heard them all: I need the money; I only started a year ago; I like my desk buddy; there are no jobs out there; it's only work; it's just not a good time to leave; what if the new job is no better?; I have responsibilities; I have no skills; maybe it's me; maybe if I just ignore it and get my work done, it will improve; I feel loyal to the company; I'll feel like a failure if I quit. The excuses are unlimited.

Exercise 31
DREAM JOB VISUALISATION

When I first started doing this exercise, I would get bogged down in the logistics of this dream job. Big mistake! You know by now that when it comes to manifesting, specifics just fence us in. So don't worry about your current skill set, don't focus on corporate ladders and don't get too concerned if the exact role that you want doesn't currently exist. Just dream big.

If you could do or be anything in your career, what would that be? Write it down in one of the following ways:

☽ Write a job description for your dream role and your dream company.

☽ Write a summary of your dream business.

This exercise gives you something to aim for. Even if it feels unachievable right now, you're cracking open a window to let a little possibility, hope and potential in.

But if you aren't happy in your job, then it isn't your truth, so it's time to drop the excuses and take a look at the predicament you're currently in.

Feelings

Now that you're a little clearer on what it is about work that leaves you feeling dissatisfied, or worse, makes you miserable, it's time to focus on exactly what feelings you're vibrating at work. The old you may have written a pros and cons list to help you determine your next move. But you've come a long way since then, so I want you to try something new and write a list that focuses on comparing high and low vibrations.

If you're mostly in a low vibrational state when at work, you'll probably find that those low vibrations ripple out into other areas of your life. Because when you vibrate on a low frequency, it pulls you out of alignment, and when you're out of alignment with your authenticity, opportunities rarely present themselves (we'll explore this more in the next chapter).

But know this: a workplace doesn't have to necessarily be toxic for it to take up valuable energy. It could just be boring as all hell. Sometimes, I find boredom even more energetically draining. The more time our energy is being drained, the less energy we have to put into creating and manifesting.

So now the next thing you need to ask yourself is *why* you're feeling like this. Is it specific projects, certain clients, your relationship with your colleagues, or perhaps negativity trickling down from upper management? If you're feeling a certain way because of people, remember that another person can't *make* you feel anything. You always have a choice about how you want to feel, though not necessarily about who you get to work with.

Exercise 32

WHAT IS YOUR WORK FREQUENCY?

Let's go back to your current work situation and examine what vibrational frequency you're currently sitting in. Remember, vibrations are just feelings.

☾ On an average day, how does being at work and producing the work that you do make you feel? If you have several different jobs, separate them out and write about them one at a time.

☾ Now take a sheet of paper and draw a line lengthways down the centre of the page. On one side, write all of the low vibrational feelings you feel at work (e.g. fear, dread, anxiety, boredom, guilt, sadness, dissatisfaction, despondency and failure). On the other side, write all of the high vibrational feelings you experience at work (e.g. happiness, joy, excitement, motivation, inspiration, hope, expansiveness and abundance).

☾ Now compare the two sides of the page. Overall, what vibrational state do you exist in? High or low?

I get it (trust me). You spend so much time with these people that if you don't get along with your clients, colleagues or bosses, it starts to affect you energetically. If you had the choice, you would choose to only surround yourself with people who are on a similar frequency to you. I mean, you could ask HR to make that a prerequisite next time they hire someone, or you could just decide to choose your level of engagement with them.

Colleagues' personal lives, their own work issues, office gossip or any other type of low vibrational state can be huge energy zappers at work, but this applies to all kinds of engagement at work. People can subconsciously (and sometimes consciously) leak their energy everywhere, so if you're not protecting your own energy, you become collateral damage.

A great exercise I do when I want to protect my energy from being affected by others is to stand with my feet firmly on the earth. I then reach down to my feet and energetically pull a zip from my toes to the crown of my head—the zip helps me visualise a protective barrier, but you might like to try visualising a bubble or a cloak.

My intention when doing this is to contain all of my energy inside this zipped zone and keep everyone else's energy on the outside. By now you know the power of holding an intention, and this exercise allows you to set an intention around how your energy is affected by other people and situations.

Exercise 33
CATCHING OTHER PEOPLE'S VIBES

Take the time to write down what low vibrations you may be taking on from the people around you. Not what they're making you feel but *how* you feel after engaging with them.

What high vibrations do you take on from certain people at work?

Perhaps you have a certain colleague who always makes you feel motivated, or a client who shows their appreciation for the work that you do. Spend more time engaging with these people.

Exercise 34
FEEL INTO YOUR
DREAM ROLE

With the last exercise fresh in your mind, I want you to now concentrate on what your ideal work vibrations would be. Again, don't focus on the details like roles, tasks, projects or people; I just want you to focus on feelings.

Imagine you are in your dream job right now (the one you mapped out in Exercise 31). How does it feel when you are at work? How do you feel when you look at your email signature and see your name next to your ideal job title? What does having a team or a boss that respects you feel like? What feelings surface each morning when you rock up at work? And when people ask you what you do for a living, what high vibrations seep from your pores?

Okay, so now you have two options: you can either work on raising those high vibrational feelings you just listed in your current work situation so that you are able to thrive at work, or you can accept that the feelings you're longing to cultivate and immerse yourself in cannot exist in your current role.

I want you to be crystal clear on which option you want to go with before we move forward. You deserve to spend your time in a high vibrational force field. The universe will support you to do this, but the more excuses you make for why you can't leave your job or make improvements to it, the more the universe will hear that you don't think you're worthy of anything better.

Exercise 35

SET INTENTIONS FOR YOUR CAREER

Now that you know what kind of work you desire and how you
want to feel when you're doing that work, it's time to set yourself
one or two intentions around your career. Remember to not only
write the intention in the present tense, but also how you will
feel about it.

These intentions might look something like this:

☾ *I attract clients who pay me generously for doing*
easeful and enjoyable work. It makes me feel confident,
safe and joyful.

☾ *I thrive in a career that I'm excited to show up for*
each day. It makes me feel inspired, motivated
and proud.

I set weekly work intentions for myself as part of how I run my business.
For example:

I have sold 25 tickets to Lunar Nights this week. This makes me
feel accomplished, motivated and safe.

I have signed three new clients this week. This makes me feel
proud, abundant and expansive.

Actions

Career shifts and changes take courage. Trust me, I get it! As mentioned, I've changed careers several times. But now that you've taken the time to reflect on your current job and the career you desire to have, it's important that you are able to take action from that place of awareness. Before you lies opportunity, potential and infinite possibility. Consider this your permission slip from the universe to be anything and do anything that your heart desires. Simply by shifting your mindset and determining how it is you want to feel at work (which you've just nailed), you're halfway there. Now it's time to tackle the 'you-doing-the-things' bit, i.e. the action.

Let's start by looking at values, priorities and passions in the workplace.

Exercise 36
WHAT'S IMPORTANT TO YOU AT WORK?

☾ List the values that are important to you in the workplace (e.g. honesty, integrity, community, progression, appreciation etc).

☾ What takes priority for you when it comes to job satisfaction? Is it creative expression, financial reward, autonomy, flexible working hours or commissions?

☾ What are you passionate about? These things don't necessarily have to be work-related, but they can be a good indication of things you love that could be incorporated in your dream job.

Okay, I've split the action part of the equation into two choose-your-own-adventure options: Option 1 is for you if you've decided to stay in your current job; Option 2 is for you if you're outta there!

OPTION 1: IMPROVING THE VIBRATIONAL FREQUENCY OF YOUR CURRENT JOB

You know enough about how energy works now to realise that if you constantly repeat thoughts and feelings that are counterintuitive and counterproductive, work is going to be harder and more draining for you.

Remember, you have a choice when it comes to all of the above, but sometimes it takes practising conscious action in order to implement it. If you sit next to someone in the office who drains your energy, talk to your manager or HR about moving desks. If your boss manages you in a way that affects your performance, request a meeting or bring it up at your next review. A good manager will want you to feel supported at work so that you can work to the best of your abilities. If they don't, perhaps it's not the right environment for you. It all comes back to what you believe you deserve and what you believe you're worthy of.

OPTION 2: SEE YA LATER, TOXICITY!

If you've made the decision to leave your job, first of all, go you! That decision takes courage and belief in yourself. Now, let's get you a new job, shall we?

Making the decision to leave a job is never easy; there are many unknowns. I have left jobs not knowing what my next move would be, and I have also left jobs fully prepared, with another one lined up. The latter situation makes for a more easeful exit, but sometimes an opportunity will only present itself when one door closes.

Exercise 37

MAKE YOUR JOB WORK FOR YOU

Knowing that you have made a conscious choice to stay in your job and make it work better for you, ask yourself some questions so you can start identifying ways that you can start improving your work life.

☾ **Can I identify my thought patterns and limiting beliefs (or excuses, as we labelled them earlier) around my work environment and then change those and my potential to thrive in this job?** By not indulging in counterproductive thoughts such as 'I hate my boss' or 'this task is below me', you'll have more energy to not take the things your boss says personally, and get through the menial tasks faster to make space for the activities you do enjoy at work.

☾ **What feelings do I desire to cultivate in this situation?** List all of the feelings you would like to feel in your current job, and set aside time each day (I recommend 2 minutes on your way to work) to actively tap into these feelings.

☾ **What action steps can I take to improve my situation?** Write an action step you can take this week, this month and perhaps long-term (if you see yourself there for a while) to put you in alignment with the job you're excited to thrive at!

Whichever option you choose, make sure you're very clear about what kind of job you want. We worked on this earlier in Exercise 31 when you visualised your dream job. Being clear about what you want is very important, otherwise you might just end up in the exact same situation.

Same room, different paint. Once you are clear about your desires, make sure you're connecting with the vibrations you want to feel in this new role, which you determined in Exercise 34 on ideal work vibrations.

It's time to take action.

Let's start simple

★ Start actively looking for jobs (it's alarming how many people who are miserable in their current role don't do this).

★ Talk to people in the industry you want to work in. Ask them to connect you with people who might be able to help you.

★ Tidy up your résumé and your LinkedIn profile and, while you're at it, all of your social-media accounts. They check them, trust me.

Step it up a notch

★ Write a cover letter for your ideal job, outlining why you are the perfect candidate for the role. Actively writing this letter as if the job already exists creates a vibrational frequency around it.

★ If your dream is to have your own business, write the mission statement for that business. Try putting a business plan together.

★ Create a vision board for your dream job. My vision boards always include vibrant pictures and words that evoke the vibrations I want to create. Why not stick your cover letter up there while you're at it? Put your vision board somewhere you'll see it every day. I once stuck mine up on a pinboard above my desk at a job I was desperate to get out of (I know, cheeky!).

★ Ensure that your thoughts, feelings and actions are all aligned with this dream job. This means your words, too. Quit saying there are no good jobs out there, or that you'll never be able to find that kind of role.

Faith

Just like every other thing I've taught you how to manifest, manifesting your ideal career comes down to believing that you can—that you're worthy and that you bloody well deserve to enjoy the work that you do. If this concept is keeping you stuck, I encourage you to revisit Chapter 9 to address any limiting beliefs that may be preventing you from enjoying what you do for a living.

Be confident in the knowledge that the perfect job for you will not pass you by. But if you're not willing to go after it, it's not going to come looking for you. You must be active in your search for a job and then have faith that the right job for you will present itself.

Rejections from jobs you thought were 'the one' mean those jobs were not meant for you. Remember that nanny job in London that fell through? I was so grateful I didn't get that job in the end, even though I was heartbroken at the time. That job was not meant for me. When you walk into job interviews, have faith that if you're the right person for the role then the job will absolutely be offered to you. As long as you're showing up as the most authentic version of yourself, there is no reason you won't get the job (if it's meant for you). If you don't, it's because something better is on the way.

Faith comes in really handy when it comes to putting yourself out there for a job. Whether it's cold-calling a company you want to work for or applying for a job you're not entirely qualified for, do it with the confidence that your action will either get you into a role that is perfect for you or it will prove fruitless, which means it wasn't right for you in the first place.

Trusting the timing of job opportunities is also something to consider. If you're taking all the right action steps and there are still no roles showing up, perhaps there are still lessons to be learned in your current job. Just like twin-flame relationships, certain jobs force us to grow (but not at the expense of your mental health).

I left a job at the height of my publishing career to work in hospitality for a few months. I took an enormous pay cut and had a lot of naysayers telling me I was crazy, but doing this helped me reconnect with the vibrations I valued most: connection, joy, fun, laughter and freedom. Once I was able to get myself back to a high vibrational state, I was able to start manifesting what I really wanted—my own successful business.

This brings me back to my food business. You know, the one I started to resent that forced me to live off peanut butter toast. I knew I wasn't done with food; I had just lost the passion for it. The high vibrations it once offered me had disappeared, and I yearned to have them back. So I made some changes. First, I looked at what specifically was not working for me anymore. It turned out I was working way too many hours on certain parts of the business for not much financial return, and exerting myself physically in other parts of the business. This imbalance was burning me out completely.

After reviewing what wasn't working and what parts of the business I'd be happy to never do again, I took a look at the parts of the business I still really enjoyed. I then created intentions around what I wanted to create more of and started saying no to the things that didn't keep me high vibin'. I got super picky about the clients I took on, I began catering for retreats rather than one-off events and I stopped developing recipes for celebrities who took all the recognition for the hours I spent slaving over a hot stove (because, resentment). And what do you know? I got my groove back! More of the clients and projects I wanted started flooding my inbox.

CHAPTER 13

Manifesting Opportunity

I don't believe in luck, and I'm a bit of a sceptic when it comes to coincidences. I believe that when you favour alignment over chaos, and can stand in your own authenticity, doors open, paths clear and opportunities present themselves in fortunate, surprising and often miraculous ways, except there are no miracles involved. YOU made it happen just by being you and giving a toss about your own vibrations.

WHAT DOES BEING IN ALIGNMENT FEEL LIKE?

Great question. 'To be in alignment' is a zeitgeisty phrase often used interchangeably with 'being in flow' or 'stepping into your authenticity'. But what do these phrases actually mean? And what exactly is aligning?

First of all, as far as the spiritual world is concerned, I'm not sure 'alignment' was coined by anyone in particular, so it's open to interpretation. I'll tell you how I feel when I'm in alignment, and you see if you resonate with it. Alignment, for me, is more of a feeling than a set of physical and material criteria; it feels expansive and effortless, and resistance falls away. Puzzle pieces land and fit with ease and grace. It's having a deep connection with self and a deep sense of knowing that your intuition is guiding you into growth with every choice you make.

When I'm in alignment, creativity blooms and high vibrations like joy, happiness and love are easily accessible and feel like my natural state of being. I have boundless energy and nothing seems impossible—in fact, everything is filled with infinite potential. When you feel this way, the alignment that's taking place is between you, your higher self and universal consciousness. It feels as if you are on purpose and exactly where you're meant to be.

However, all of this comes with a caveat: being in alignment *doesn't* mean there won't be work. It also doesn't mean life will be free of overwhelm or stresses. There will likely still be obstacles and longer paths to venture down. I think that past definitions of 'alignment' have forgotten to mention that.

When I moved out of my apartment of thirteen years, I was a week out from the deadline for the first draft of this book. The universe had sent me a bazillion signs and synchronicities telling me that this was the time to move. Whenever I closed a door a new one would open, and the more plans I made to move the more expansive I felt, but geez, it was inconvenient timing.

With two chapters still to write and a whole manuscript to review, I spent my days writing and my nights packing. I had several panic attacks the more the boxes piled up around me, and the walls felt like they were closing in. But I did it. I pushed through because although it was overwhelming and stressful, it never felt constrictive or like I wasn't doing the right thing. Intuitively, I knew that everything was playing out exactly as it should be.

To be in alignment is to be vibrating on a frequency that aligns you with your purpose, and this alone is enough to manifest opportunity. To be out of alignment is to ignore, resist or be ignorant to the parts of you that take you away from your soul's purpose.

I can think of countless examples of this in my own life: relationships I stayed in because I didn't want to 'fail' at them; jobs I didn't leave because, on paper, I hadn't been there long enough; friendships I forced even though we'd grown apart; apartments I stayed in for thirteen years because I felt comfortable and safe; and red flags I ignored in all areas of my life because I'd rather suffer the consequences than disappoint someone else.

When you're out of alignment, your vibrational frequency becomes compromised. Your actions start to contradict your intentions, and that's bloody confusing to the universe. And this is why the action part is so integral to the equation. It's all very well *knowing* what you desire, but when you step out of alignment with the vibrations of that desire, things get real hard.

Being out of alignment feels like climbing a mountain with gale-force winds hitting you squarely in the face. No matter how hard you force and push, you can't get any closer to the top of that mountain. I often liken it to running on a treadmill—it doesn't matter how fast you run, you're still in the exact same position.

Your feelings are your biggest ally when it comes to detecting when you are out of alignment. Fear and anxiety overcome you, your intuition screams, 'This isn't right. Abort! Abort! Abort!' Your energy is zapped, you feel overwhelmed to the point of exhaustion, you find it difficult to tap into higher vibrations and you feel restless and unsatisfied. In the worst-case scenario, you begin to feel nothing. You become numb.

In a nutshell, it's like this:

Alignment = feels good and expansive
Out of alignment = feels tough and constrictive

Ooh, sounds great!
So how do I become more aligned?

Feeling aligned is a never-ending personal journey. You don't just find yourself aligned one day and then that's the end of the story. Nope! It's a process of constantly checking in with yourself by asking questions like, 'Is this right for me?' If the answer is no, then it's about adjusting to get back on course.

Be constantly curious about yourself. When making a decision, ask yourself a bunch of nosy questions: What do I desire? What do I need? Does this serve me? Do I want more of this? Do I want less of this? Answer honestly.

Take responsibility for your actions. The only person who can impact your life profoundly is you. So if there are things that are pulling you away from your authenticity and shifting you into lower vibrations, then step up and make the necessary changes.

Focus on joy. I have found that as long as I constantly seek joy, it's very hard for me to become misaligned. I ask myself, 'Does this bring me joy?' If the answer is no, I ask, 'What does this bring me?' If it's not another high vibration, then I find another option. It's as simple as that. If you don't think you can do this, I guarantee there's a limiting belief standing in your way.

Listen to your intuition. We've addressed intuition several times in this book, and it really is the control centre for staying in alignment with yourself and your soul purpose. Your intuition will never lead you down the wrong path. Even if it might feel like a more convoluted, windy route, it's all part of your soul's growth. If you can trust in it implicitly, your intuition will always keep you aligned.

Stay accountable to the Manifestation Equation. I find staying in alignment a more easeful endeavour when I am implementing the teachings of manifestation. The whole point of the Manifestation Equation is to align you with the things that you want to create in your life by encouraging you to vibrate on the same frequency as them. By being mindful of your thoughts, choosing high vibrational feelings, taking conscious action and trusting in yourself and the universe, you are pretty much the most aligned one human can be.

This is how you'll be able to manifest opportunity in your life. Not through luck and not by coincidence, but because you're radiating the essence of your highest self at all times. That's not to say you won't slip in and out of alignment, but it's all about having the awareness and curiosity to bring yourself back.

As we've already discovered, things in your life aren't happening to you, you are making them happen. It's not coincidence, luck or even chance. Opportunities arise in your life because of the actions that you take to make them happen.

HOW OPPORTUNITY CAN MANIFEST

Anything you are able to manifest in your life begins as an opportunity. Love, money, career, holiday, car, kismet encounters, friendships, clients, ticket sales ... the list is endless. But unless you take action on an opportunity, the manifestation is void.

I thrive on finding opportunity in everything, and it's probably the reason people deem me so lucky. But in order to be presented with an opportunity, you need to be able to recognise one when it shows up. This means deconstructing your perception of how something should look or present itself to you. It's crucial that you look outside the box, remove your blinkers and see things from all angles. The universe is full of infinite possibility, potential and opportunity, but unless you are open and willing to receive it, it will pass you by.

Here are some ways opportunity might show up:

★ You're seated next to a stranger on a long-haul flight, and they strike up a conversation with you. You could instantly dismiss it, and excuse yourself by feigning sleep, but perhaps this is an opportunity to learn something new. Perhaps they might offer you a potential lead on something you're trying to achieve.

★ You feel a sudden impulse to go to a different coffee shop, walk an alternate route or stop at a new grocery store, and this puts you face to face with an ex-colleague who gives you a lead on a new position at your dream company. It's up to you whether you follow it up.

★ The landlord just raised the rent on your apartment and you're trying to decide your next move, knowing that you can't really afford to stay without feeling constricted by the increase. That night, you're on Facebook and see that a friend is looking for someone to take over the lease of their perfect apartment the week your rent is due to increase. This might seem like a coincidence and divine timing, but this is an opportunity for you to avoid the stress of struggling financially by staying where you are.

★ You tell yourself you want to start going to yoga, but you're worried you'll be the worst yogi in the room. While scrolling through social media that night, you see the yoga studio down the road is offering a six-week beginners' course. Coincidence? I think not.

Each one of these examples requires action, and without that piece of the puzzle, they're just opportunities. In my life, I look at opportunities like these as little signs from the universe—confirmation that I'm on the right path. They're not an external happenstance; they are the result of your vibrational frequency and authenticity. I can't stress enough how much your life will change for the better once you can wrap your noggin' around this concept.

When I decided to do yoga-teacher training, I was running my business and had expenses coming out of the proverbial. I just didn't have $5,000 to fork out for the training, even though I knew it would enhance the work I was already doing in my business. So for months, I set the following intention:

> I have completed my 200-hour yoga-teacher training
> and am now a qualified yoga teacher. I feel accomplished,
> credible and excited.

I didn't worry about the specifics of how, when or where, I just stuck with the intention. If I'm being honest, I assumed I would manifest the money to pay for it, but it worked out very differently. Once day, while scrolling through social media, I spotted a post from the yoga school I wanted to do my training with. They were advertising their upcoming training program, and in very fine print underneath, it said, 'Ask us about our work trade offer'! I messaged them straightaway, and within the next week I was offering my digital and editing expertise in exchange for a spot on the next part-time yoga-teacher training program.

Opportunities are out there! You just need to keep your eyes and your mind open. Every golden opportunity seemingly handed to you was created for you by you. Period. This is the gift of manifestation.

PUT YOURSELF SMACK-BANG IN THE MIDDLE OF OPPORTUNITY'S PATH

'Knock, knock.'
'Who's there?'
'Opportunity …'
'Oh, hey! Come on in.'

This could definitely happen, but just like the soulmate who's unlikely to waltz into your lounge room on a Friday night, sometimes opportunity requires you to put some legwork into finding it. It's very easy to get caught up in the romanticism of destiny, and think, if it's meant to be, it will be, but that doesn't mean you shouldn't actively be out in the world seeking opportunity.

Seeking opportunity could look like this:

★ Attending a networking event to attract new clients to your business.
★ Saying yes to invitations to friends' parties so you can meet new people.
★ Inquiring about payment plans for online courses.

- ★ Going on that dating app! (Okay, I know I've mentioned this a few times. I swear they're not paying me to spruik them.)
- ★ Contacting your dream company on LinkedIn, and sending them your résumé.

If you're in a constant state of waiting to receive, you throw off the balance of the Manifestation Equation. Remember, you must practise action and faith together. Take the action to seek opportunity and have faith that the opportunity will present itself. And if it doesn't? Well then, and only then, perhaps it's not meant to be. See the difference?

GET CRYSTAL CLEAR ABOUT YOU WANT

I run a manifestation-mentoring practice, and one of the biggest struggles my clients have is getting clarity around what they want their future to look like. It's all very well to hate your job, but what would you rather be doing? Only when you can get clear on where you're headed are you able to see opportunity when it presents itself. And it's not only good to get clear about your future, it's also helpful to get clear on your present circumstances.

Instead of writing pros and cons lists, I encourage my clients to write a low vibrations and high vibrations list for the area they are trying to manifest in—as you did in Exercise 32 for your work situation. I encourage you to write this type of list because it can give you a really clear picture of where your energy is going, and this is very helpful when looking at your relationships, work, home life ... any area you choose to apply it to.

If making this list reveals that the low vibrational feelings are dominant, it's time to make some changes.

Once you're clear on your current circumstance, it's time to get clear on what you want to create more of in your life. Without clarity, how will you be able to apply everything you've learned about manifestation? Remember, this isn't about specifics, so if getting caught up in the details is preventing you from seeing things clearly, focus instead on how you want to *feel* in the future.

Only when we're clear about the high vibrations we want to radiate can we identify and take full advantage of opportunities when they present themselves.

CHAPTER 14

Ritual, Sacred Space and Your Manifestation Toolkit

I know I promised you less woo-woo, but indulge me a little, won't you? Because while crystals, oracle cards, white sage and essential oils won't manifest *for* you, they can be wonderful tools for creating an anchor point and a sacred space that enhances your manifestation practice. And using these tools in specific ways and within certain spaces can enhance their potency even further.

RITUAL

Ritual has become a lost part of modern culture. Sure, we each have our little routines: morning coffee, gym, Sunday coastal walks, switching the lights on and off three times before leaving the house (no, just me?), but even so, the primal importance that ritual plays in our lives has been largely forgotten.

Throughout history, rituals have served as links to our ethnicity, religion and ancestral traditions, but rituals can also be created, expressed and practised as a way to connect and develop our own personal identity.

For me, ritual is a spiritual anchor. It creates structure, motivation and purpose around an experience as well as a sense of familiarity, significance and energetic intention. The most potent ritual is one that holds personal significance for you. It might take a little trial and error to feel into what resonates with you, but the end reward is worth it.

There is no right or wrong when it comes to creating a ritual. If it feels good, expansive and serves you in some way, then it's perfect.

And although ritual requires a certain level of consistency, you should never feel bound by it. So change it up however you need to in each and every moment. The following are some of the ways that I incorporate ritual into my manifestation practice.

Meditating and visualisation

I studied in the Vedic meditation tradition, which uses mantra to calm the mind, and encourages you to meditate for twenty minutes in the morning and twenty minutes in the afternoon. But honestly, I'm lucky if I get five minutes in each day. If you're only going to meditate for five minutes a day, you want to get the most out of it, right? So I use those five minutes, first thing when I wake up or just before I fall asleep, to visualise what I want to manifest and tap into the high vibrations associated with them. If you take only one practice from this chapter, please make it this one ... it's life changing.

Manifesting by the moon

I spoke briefly of the power of following the moon on page 110 in relation to the Law of Rhythm and the natural ebb and flow of all universal cycles. I set my entire manifestation practice around the lunar cycle. All eight phases of the moon support the growth of my intentions and give me a certain level of accountability because following the moon provides specific anchor points (the eight different phases). I set intentions on a new moon and release any obstacles on a full moon. The month's worth of dates help to keep you accountable to your practice. And if you fall out of step with it for whatever reason, you have a chance to get back on track the next month when the cycle repeats.

MANIFESTING BY THE MOON CHART

◯	**New Moon**	I like to think of the new moon as an empty vessel. It's the perfect time to fill up on all of the intentions you have for the month ahead. Plant seeds, write down new ideas and begin fresh projects.
☽	**Waxing Crescent**	Take some time to explore your intentions. How do they feel in your heart space? Why these intentions? What do they mean to you? Connect with your intentions on a deeper level.
◗	**First Quarter**	Take inspired action towards your intentions. What actions could you take over the next few days to be one step closer to manifesting your intentions?
◗	**Waxing Gibbous**	You are being tested to stay on course with your productivity before you switch to a yin energy. Can you observe your intentions rather than control them?
●	**Full Moon**	This marks the waning phase of the lunar cycle. It is the perfect time to trust, surrender, release and let go. The best way to let go is to practise forgiveness regularly. Take this time to release the things that are no longer serving you and to forgive the people and experiences that have hurt you (including yourself).
☾	**Waning Gibbous**	Instead of resisting, I encourage you to relax into the slower vibes this phase conjures up. It's the perfect time to turn inwards and practise gratitude.
◖	**Third Quarter**	This phase can often feel like an 'in limbo' energy. It's a good time to reflect on limiting beliefs. Are you stuck in patterns that are preventing your intentions from manifesting?
☾	**Waning Crescent**	Take rest before the yang energy of the new moon hits in the following days. The best way to make the most of this phase is to 100 per cent release anything that you don't wish to take with you into the new lunar cycle.

If this is something you are keen to get on board with, there are a tonne of resources on my website, or you can follow the very simple chart on page 303. Lunar energy supports manifestation and, like I said, it's great for accountability, but in no way is it a mandatory part of manifestation. Think of it as an adornment rather than a necessity.

Journaling

Each calendar year I start a new intentions journal, and I encourage you to do the same. Having all of your intentions in one place allows you to reflect on them regularly and see which intentions have manifested and which intentions might need a few tweaks.

I also use this same journal to record all of my free-writing exercises. I'll often free-write in the morning, depicting my ideal life in the present tense—similar to the free-writing exercise I encouraged you to do on page 54 before you set your five intentions.

When all of our manifestations are recorded in the one place, I believe that the journal itself takes on its own high-vibrational frequency and becomes a powerful tool in its own right.

SETTING UP A SACRED SPACE

While meditation, the moon and journaling are useful suggestions, they are by no means mandatory to successful manifestation. However, I do believe that creating a physical space for you to explore your practice is paramount. By now you know the power of energy and vibrations, so don't you think it makes sense to have a space that's dedicated to cultivating and nurturing those high vibrations?

Creating a sacred space is a very personal experience. For me, this space needs to be comfortable (I like lots of cushions), free from clutter and have adjustable lighting (I like mood lighting when meditating and brighter light for journaling). Most importantly, it needs to be a space that is only used for my spiritual practices (i.e. it shouldn't double as your dining room or your kid's romper room). You might prefer your sacred space to be outdoors; if so, that's absolutely fine. There really are no rules; it just needs to feel sacred to YOU.

What happens in this sacred space?

GREAT question! My sacred space is where I meditate, set my intentions, feel into my vibrations, plan action steps and often daydream over a cup of tea. I absolutely do not scroll through social media, send emails or mull over a to-do list in this space ... because, sacred! Over time, what happens in this space is that you create a force field of high vibrations. I guarantee that each time you visit it, you will find it easier to connect with what it is that you want to make happen.

Cleansing your sacred space

I'm a serial cleanser. Before I sit down to work, after I clean the house, before I cook dinner, when I have friends over, after they leave, when I break up with a partner, invite a new partner in ... you get the picture. I may be a little excessive, but there is definitely no harm in it (don't worry, I've checked). But cleansing a space doesn't mean removing surface dirt and grime with an all-purpose cleaner—it's more about clearing out energetic dust and old vibrational remnants from a space in order to make room for fresh new energy and positive new vibrations.

I use two different materials to cleanse and 'smudge' a room, depending on what I feel drawn to that day. Again there is no right or wrong.

White sage smudge stick: You can purchase these in most health food or spiritual stores these days. The one I'm currently using is a mixture of white sage, rosemary, lavender and rose. White sage has been used for centuries in the Native American traditions to cleanse, clear and protect a space. It is believed that the smoke attaches to unwanted energies and clears them out. Think of it as a spiritual 'spring clean'.

Palo santo: Also known as 'holy wood', palo santo has been used for centuries by the Incas and natives of the Andes as a spiritual tool for purifying and protecting a space. Due to over harvesting, palo santo trees are now on the endangered species list. If you already have some at home, use it only for special occasions and perhaps look at alternative native woods and herbs to cleanse with instead.

> **Warning**
>
> This activity will set off smoke alarms, so be conscious of this when smudging a room fitted with an alarm.
>
>

The technique for cleansing or smudging is the same whether you use white sage or palo santo. Eventually, you can come up with your own style of ritual, but to get you started, this is how I do it. You'll also need:

★ a lighter or matches (or barbecue lighter, if you're stuck); and
★ an abalone shell, ceramic plate or a small vessel of sand.

1. Light the smudge stick or palo santo and allow it to burn for about one minute before blowing out the flame. It will begin to smoke.

2. Start by cleansing yourself. Using a feather or your hand, gently fan the smoke from your feet up to your crown, and then back down. As you do so, have the intention of clearing and protecting your entire being.

3. To cleanse the space, move clockwise around the room, gently waving smoke into the air. Again, you can just hold the intention of clearing and protecting the space in your mind, or you can say an affirmation as you walk around the room. I say something along the lines of, 'May this space be clear of energies that will not serve me in the highest and best way. May space be created for fresh, new and vibrant energy to enter my life.'

4. Trace the edges of doorways and windows, and be sure to spend some time getting into the corners and crevices of a room (where any energy can become stagnant).

5. Once you have finished, extinguish the smudge stick or palo santo in either your abalone shell, ceramic plate or vessel of sand.

ASSEMBLING YOUR MANIFESTATION TOOLKIT

I built my manifestation toolkit up over time. Yours might look very different to mine, but it will consist of adornments to your manifestation practice—things that add a level of sacredness and ceremony. I travel A LOT for work, and I take my toolkit with me wherever I go. Toiletries? Check! Undies? Check! Manifestation toolkit? Check! You might like to put everything in a beautiful wooden box to keep your collection safe and sacred.

Oracle and tarot cards

When I was a little girl, my mum worked as a tarot reader and psychic from our home. (I know, right?!) To be honest with you, as a child, this freaked me out! But when she gave me my first deck of oracle cards at fifteen, I started to come around to the idea of using them. My own deck empowered me! It became a wonderful supplementary tool for developing and trusting my intuition by offering gentle guidance and direction that I had the option to take or leave.

When I turned thirty, Mum passed down my great grandmother's Rider-Waite tarot deck (the most traditional type of tarot cards). Three generations of women in my family before me had used this deck as a self-guidance tool, and I now use it not only for my own guidance, but also to read for other people, too.

I am of the firm belief that both oracle and tarot cards work with the Law of Vibration. We are drawn to particular cards in the deck because we are vibrating on a similar frequency to them. While many of us rely heavily on what the tarot books say when interpreting the meaning of the cards, I like to use my intuition first. Using your intuition often is the best way to strengthen it. It's not about guessing what the book says, it's about interpreting the meaning of the card and how it applies to your particular circumstances by using your own inner guidance.

While everybody uses cards differently, I thought it might be helpful to share how I incorporate them into my manifestation ritual. You can use any deck of tarot or oracle cards you like. I tend to use my Rider-Waite tarot deck, but use whatever you're drawn to.

It's very important (especially if other people have been in contact with your deck) that you cleanse the cards before using them. If you're the only one using them, you don't need to worry about cleansing them every time unless they're brand new or you haven't touched them for a while and they've been sitting in a dusty drawer.

Cleansing the cards: Place the full deck in your non-dominant hand. Using your dominant hand, tap the deck three times, visualising any negative energy leaving the deck. Then touch each card in the deck one by one with your dominant hand to inject your energy into the cards. (Note: You can also cleanse a deck using a smudge stick or palo santo by wafting the smoke over and around the deck and holding the intention to cleanse it.)

Drawing your cards: There are many different ways to do this, but this is what I do when I set intentions (usually on the new moon). Shuffle the deck well (intuitively, you'll know when to stop). Using your non-dominant hand, split the deck three times. Restack the deck and then split it again into two piles. Place the bottom pile on top and then draw three cards from the top of the deck.

I use these three cards as guidance around my intentions. Often I'll decide which card will correspond to which area of my life before drawing them. For example, I'll decide that the first card will be for love, the second for money and the third for health. Again, you decide what feels best for you. I try to stick to drawing just three cards, otherwise I find myself pulling until I draw a card I like (FYI that's cheating!). I write them in my journal next to my intentions. I will also make sure I date the reading and any other significant factors, such as the moon phase, the season and where I am in my cycle (again, personal choice) etc.

Crystals

Back to my hippie-dippy mum for a moment (love you, Mum!). Our house was adorned with crystals. I mean, they were just part of the decor, I never really thought twice about them. I always had crystals by my bed, under my pillow, in the bath, guarding my bedroom door, in my schoolbag. Everywhere really.

Today I'm the same. My house is overflowing with them, and I pretty much always have a rose quartz tumble stone in my bra, a citrine in my wallet, quartz wands in the kitchen, a quartz sphere on my desk and a big chunky amethyst by the television to ground the frequently flighty energy of my lounge room.

Crystals have been used for centuries to heal and bring balance. They work through energetic vibration. Each crystal has its own benefits, but I always tell people not to get too caught up in that. Just pop a crystal in your hand, close your eyes and feel into its energy. You'll know if it's the right one for you.

If you're interested in learning more about crystals, there are lots of great resources online. To get you started, these are the crystals I find most beneficial for manifestation.

Rose quartz: The crystal of pure and unconditional love (hello, soulmate). Rose quartz is the stone of the heart, and while it's wonderful at supporting relationships, its true superpower is that it can help you cultivate more self-love. Place it by your bed, in the relationship corner of your home (this is a feng shui thing, and trust me, it's worth looking into!) or wear it close to your heart. As I mentioned, I like to place a rose quartz tumble stone in my bra. This also makes for a fun surprise when you get to second base with your lover. *Creepy wink*

Amethyst: This is the crystal of spirituality and wisdom (hello, universal faith). It also acts as a personal bodyguard by protecting you from negative energy and transmuting that energy into love. It is very calming and soothing for the mind, making it perfect for incorporating into a meditation practice. It is highly regarded as the stone of spiritual wisdom, facilitating deeper access to your intuition and psychic gifts.

Citrine: The crystal of abundance and regeneration (hello, money maker). Citrine also increases personal power, boosts self-esteem and activates creativity. I like to have citrine around my workspace and in my wallet. If you struggle with aligning your thoughts and expressing your feelings, it is said that citrine can help you overcome those difficulties.

Clear quartz: This is great at amplifying vibrations, which makes it a perfect crystal to use when setting intentions. I use a lot of clear quartz at my intention-setting and manifestation events to amplify the high vibrations in the room. It is also said to enhance psychic abilities, attune you to your spiritual purpose and dissolve past-life karma. It's a great crystal to have around when smashing through limiting beliefs because it clears the energy and facilitates reprogramming.

CLEANSING YOUR CRYSTALS
USING MOONLIGHT

If you're using crystals as part of your manifestation practice, it's important that you're cleansing and charging them often. Crystals absorb and retain so much energy; it's what makes them so powerful and healing. Like anything, including humans, absorbing too much of anything can begin to overload the system. The same can be said of crystals. To keep them active and working at their peak, it's important to give them a reset once a month. Cleanse your crystals with filtered water or by smudging with white sage, then pop them outside under the full moon. If you can lay them on the earth, even better, but if not a balcony or windowsill will do. It's also important to do this when you purchase or are gifted a new crystal.

PROGRAMMING YOUR CRYSTALS
WITH YOUR INTENTIONS

At every Lunar Nights event I host, I place a crystal grid at the front of the room. My intention for this grid is for it to amplify the vibrations of the conscious collective who have gathered in the space to set intentions. A shaman designed this grid specifically for this purpose, and I tell you what, it is so freaking powerful!

The grid was originally designed for me to sit in but I found the energy inside it too intense, so now I sit on the outside and experience it with everyone else in the room. If anybody ever questions the energy of crystals, I just tell them to sit next to this grid and experience its potency—it's undeniable.

Using your own crystals when setting intentions is a profoundly powerful experience. When choosing which crystals to work with, it's a good idea to make your choices based on the specific qualities of that crystal (as listed above) as well as its colour, shape or whatever it is that draws you to that crystal. Sometimes I prefer to not know what the specific qualities of a crystal are and allow my intuition to guide me.

Once you've chosen a crystal to work with, follow these steps:

1. Cleanse and clear your crystal using the methods outlined on the opposite page. It's important that the energy be clear for the new intention that you would like to set.

2. Hold the crystal in your non-dominant hand, and close your eyes. Imagine a white light emanating over the crystal in your hand, cleansing it, charging it and giving it purpose.

3. Say out loud, 'May this crystal be used for the highest good, to heal and balance with love and light.'

4. Sit with the crystal in your palm, connecting with its energy. When you feel fully plugged in, say out loud, 'My intention for this crystal is ...'

5. Sit in stillness, repeating your intention until you feel it connect with the crystal.

6. I like to revisit this once a month. I will cleanse and charge the crystal on the full moon, and connect it back to my intention the next day.

OTHER WAYS TO MANIFEST USING CRYSTALS:

★ Place them over your journal to help amplify the vibrations of your intentions.

★ Hold them in your hands when doing a manifestation visualisation.

★ If you're manifesting money or career progression, try keeping your crystals on your desk or in your wallet.

★ Wear your crystals. I once had a stranger grab my hand as I was walking down the street. He said, 'You're wearing so many crystals, I can *feel* them on you.' I showed him the giant smoky quartz ring I always wear, and he said, 'Where else? I can feel them.' He was not wrong. I also had an amethyst keyring, a rose quartz in my bra, a quartz around my neck and a citrine in my wallet. He then proceeded to pull crystals out of his socks (not joking) and an array of crystals from around a chain on his neck. Crystals are powerful, my friends. Wear them with caution.

Burn, baby, burn!

Fire is a powerful force of destruction, creation, transformation and purification. It has been used across various cultures for centuries as part of core spiritual and ritual practices.

In the Native American tradition, a shamanic fire ceremony is performed to clear negative energies and any unnecessary attachments in order to make way for new energy and intentions. The Hindu tradition practises a Vedic ritual called 'havan' as an offering of worship and devotion. Indigenous Australians perform traditional Aboriginal smoking ceremonies to ward off bad spirits, pay respect to the departed, to celebrate and also to clear and heal. Esoteric Buddhists hold a goma fire ceremony to burn away the roots of suffering and also to pray for their intentions to manifest. In paganism, the celebration of Litha or Summer Solstice is often accompanied by a fire ceremony as a form of worshipping the sun.

I love incorporating fire into my manifestation ritual for reasons that mirror all of the above traditions. I've already outlined how I use burning sage or palo santo to cleanse and clear my sacred space, but I also have another ritual I perform every full moon. In order to release the things that are no longer serving me, I write them down on a piece of paper then burn that to ashes (always with the motto safety first, of course).

MANIFESTING THROUGH FIRE

Sounds pretty dramatic, doesn't it? If you would like to try a similar manifestation ritual using fire, you'll need:

★ sage or palo santo
★ a candle
★ a few pieces of paper (not a notebook)
★ a pen
★ your favourite crystal
★ a lighter or matches

Although you don't have to do this on a full moon, the lunar energy of a full moon will support this practice. Follow these steps:

1. Cleanse the space with either sage or palo santo. Simply light your cleansing tool, and smudge the space with the intention of clearing any negative or stagnant energies that may prevent the success of your releasing ritual.

2. Gather all of your supplies, and find a comfortable seat.

3. Light your candle.

4. Close your eyes and centre your energy. Bring awareness to your breath, and allow it to flow smoothly in and out of your nostrils, without any force. If you're finding it hard to settle your energy, it might help to repeat internally 'Let' on the inhale and 'Go' on the exhale.

5. Once you feel your energy has settled and you are calm, open your eyes. Remember the free-writing exercise you did before setting your intentions? This time I want you to free write about all of the things you wish to release from your life. Think big! What is no longer serving you? Just keep writing. Don't edit or pause, just allow the words to flow.

6. Read through what you've written and notice any themes or commonalities that keep showing up for you.

7. Place your crystal on top of the piece of paper. Place your left hand on your heart and your right hand on the crystal. Recite the following mantra:

I allow myself to release these things from my life. I no longer wish to carry these through with me to the next phase of the lunar cycle. I have learned the lessons and I'm ready to step into my truth and authenticity, leaving behind that which no longer serves me.

8. Now blow out the candle. This is symbolic of ceremonial endings.

9. Rip the piece of paper into pieces. Keeping the motto 'safety first' in mind, burn the paper to ashes. I like to do this in the kitchen sink, but you could throw it in a fireplace or a fire pit, if you have one.

10. Lastly, place the crystal outside in the full moonlight to cleanse and recharge it. If the moon isn't full, make sure you sage the crystal well and remember to pop it under the light of the next full moon.

Fire can be a trigger for some people, or something they associate with trauma. If this is the case for you, you'll still be able to perform this ritual with a few tweaks. In fact, when I was a kid, Mum and I would perform a similar ceremony, but instead of burning the paper we'd fold it up and pop it in the freezer! (LOL!) Apparently the cold neutralises the negative energies. Another good option is to bury it in the earth.

Essential oils

Of my five senses, I think my sense of smell is probably the strongest. This doesn't bode well for me in many circumstances—when a fellow yogi wears too much perfume, a guy on the bus forgets to apply deodorant, or that faint smell of seaweed lingers on a shoreline after a summer storm. I am convinced I smell everything a billion times stronger than the average nose (okay, maybe not a billion), but it's definitely true that smell is a visceral experience for me. It creates a clear sense of nostalgia and links me strongly to specific memories and anchor points in my life.

For this reason I love incorporating scent, and essential oils in particular, into my manifestation practice. Their scents instantly activate the feelings behind my intentions and act as a reminder of the vibrations I want to attract. Again, I urge you to use your intuition when choosing oils, but here is a rough guide to a few oils that can enhance your manifestation efforts.

For spiritual enhancement

Sandalwood brings us back to the spiritual and is perfect to use during practices that require devotion. It supports us to surrender and trust in ourselves and a higher power.

Clary sage is the oil of clarity, giving you the courage and vision to see the truth of a situation. It's wonderful at opening up your third eye and gaining a clear channel of communication between you and the universe.

Cypress is the oil of flow; it teaches the soul how to let go from past stories and move forward with trust and adaptability.

Frankincense is the oil of truth, and probably my favourite oil of all. It encourages high vibrations by allowing you to release anything that will cause you to slip into a lower vibration. It helps you to recall wisdom and knowledge, and it encourages spiritual evolution. Plus, it demolishes wrinkles. #bonus #livingproof

For self-acceptance

Patchouli brings us back into our body and physicality. It allows us to be fully present and evokes self-acceptance of our physical body. It also deepens our connection with Mother Earth and her universal cycles.

Bergamot supports us to have self-acceptance and to trust ourselves. It evokes feelings of self-love and confidence.

Grapefruit asks us to honour our body and validate and nourish ourselves.

Geranium is all about love and trust. It teaches us to be patient and tolerant with ourselves, strengthening and stabilising our connection to self.

Rose is the oil of divine love. I wear rose every day as a sweet reminder that I am love.

For uplifting vibrations

Lime helps revitalise and uplift the heart space, bringing room for light and happiness.

Wild orange is the oil of abundance and activates creativity. It promotes feelings of an infinite supply guiding us out of a scarcity mentality.

Lemongrass is a powerful energy cleanser. It can assist you to release toxicity, limiting beliefs and negative energies.

Peppermint activates joy and buoyancy in the heart. This uplifting scent can have immediate results, so use it when you feel like you need a short reprieve from an emotional slump.

For introspection

Vetiver assists us to become more grounded, centred and present, and allows us to connect with ourselves on a deep emotional level.

Cedarwood is known as the oil of community, promoting feelings of connectedness, belonging and support.

Lavender allows us to open ourselves to communication, encouraging emotional honesty within ourselves and with those around us. It also promotes a restful slumber.

Juniper berry balances between light and dark, and all the spaces between. It promotes feelings of protection, dreaming and self-awareness.

Black pepper encourages us to be open and honest. It allows us to radiate authenticity and is a great motivator.

Cardamom assists us with centring, surrendering and redirecting our energy inwards. It prompts us to take responsibility for our self and our feelings, and this invites peace, calm and a sense of control.

HOW TO USE THE OILS

There are lots of simple ways to incorporate essential oils into your manifestation practice.

Diffuser: Diffusing is a wonderful way to create an aroma in your sacred space without having to apply an oil topically. Once I have associated a certain scent with my monthly practice, I continue to diffuse that combination of oils for the month ahead.

Manifesting diffuser blend: cedarwood, clary sage, bergamot and wild orange.

Massage: Sometimes, as part of my manifestation practice and to cultivate a little self-love, I will have a hot shower or bath and apply some essential oils mixed with a carrier oil such as jojoba, almond or coconut while my skin is still damp. During my full-body self-massage, I feel into my intentions to make a connection between the aroma and my vibrational frequency.

Manifesting massage blend: jojoba, grapefruit, rose, bergamot and patchouli.

Bathing rituals: The apartment I lived in for thirteen years didn't have a bathtub. (I know! That should be illegal.) But whenever I was fortunate to be staying somewhere with a bath, I loved taking the time while soaking to get introspective and visualise my intentions as fully-fledged manifestations. Make sure you set the scene appropriately by dimming the lights, lighting some candles and closing the door so you're free from distraction. Disperse five or six drops of a single oil or your favourite blend. I also like to add a tablespoon of a carrier oil such as jojoba or almond.

Manifesting bath blend: 3 drops lavender, 2 drops juniper berry and 1 drop black pepper.

Anointing: If you're sensitive to oils I would give this one a miss, but I often anoint myself with a single oil when I want to really connect with its qualities. I will intuitively apply it wherever it feels good, but common places are between the brows (on the third eye), on my heart, behind my ears or on my pulse points. If I feel particularly anxious and unable to practise non-attachment, I will anoint the soles of my feet before bed with lavender or bergamot oil.

Inhaling: A really good on-the-go trick for reconnecting with your intentions when you find yourself floundering or having difficulty trusting in the process is opening up a bottle of essential oil and having a good old-fashioned whiff. I carry a 5 ml bottle of peppermint oil in my bag for this very reason. If you find carrying the bottle around too much, or you would prefer a blend, dot a handkerchief or tissue with the oils before leaving the house.

The most important thing when creating ritual and ceremony around your manifestation practice is to have fun with it. The process should uplift and motivate you, not feel like a chore. Be fluid with your practice but not your commitment. Consistency is key to any ritual, and the more you connect with it on a regular basis, the more powerful your manifestation practice will become.

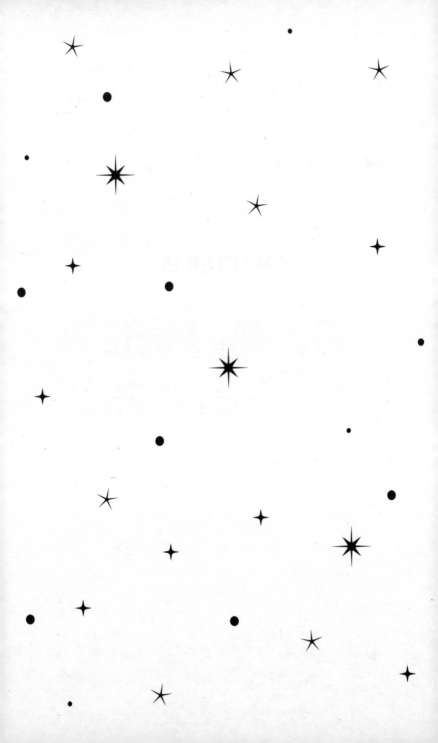

CHAPTER 15

Fly, My Little Manifester, Fly!

Is it just me, or is the final chapter of every self-help/personal development book scary AF?!

You've just devoured countless pages of poetic prose, transformative techniques, crystal-clear concepts and witty one-liners, all expertly executed in such a way that you feel like you've already upgraded as a human simply by flicking through the pages. Only now there's pressure. Now you have to actually do ALL OF THE THINGS. Holy shit!

Don't worry, I feel ya! In fact, when I was writing this book the universe quite forcefully unravelled every single area of my life, giving me the opportunity to experience the magic of the Manifestation Equation again and again. At the time I was like, 'Geez, Louise! Give a gal a break,' but as I penned each chapter (read: typed) I was presented with a corresponding lesson. Only by implementing the teachings I've shared with you in the pages of this very book was I able to wholeheartedly stand in my truth and say, 'By George, I think she's got it!' This stuff really works!

I took myself off to Bali to write the self-worth chapter, and let me tell you, after days in my swimsuit I found myself once again playing that tired old game of pull, push, rotate and lift in the mirror. The more I stared at my reflection, the deeper I began to spiral into self-doubt. 'I can't write this book. Nobody wants to hear about my boobies. How did I even get a book deal? Nobody is going to buy this, I mean, look at the size of my butt!' (As if the two are somehow connected.) So you know what I did? I recognised what was happening, and I labelled my thoughts. I yelled STOP! like a crazy woman until the pattern of thoughts exploded into tiny little pieces. I focused instead on feelings that served me and increased my self-worth rather than on feelings that wasted my energy. Instead of tugging at my saddlebags, I closed my eyes and practised deep breathing. I complimented people, I told myself (as I would a friend) that I *was* worthy and deserving, and that I *was* being the most authentic version of me, and that was why people would buy my book. By changing nothing except being extra loving towards myself during the writing process, I actually dropped five kilos (not that it was ever about that, but #bonus).

While writing the money chapter, I had three different clients cancel projects at the last minute. Money I had been counting on was suddenly no longer within my reach. Bills were piling up, expenses were due to come out of my account, and I was (casually) freaking out. I felt myself slipping back into my old money story; I became completely overwhelmed by all of my monthly expenses, and I held on tightly to the little money I did have, not trusting that more would come in. So I went through and did every single exercise I outline in the money chapter. I wrote my current money story and worked out which feelings were fuelling my financial overwhelm. I wrote out a budget to get my head around exactly where I was at financially. I paid all of the outstanding bills that I could, and I trusted in the ebb and flow of all energy by tuning back into the cyclical rhythm of my breath. And, just like I explain throughout the money chapter, as sure as money flows out it ALWAYS comes back in again, and it did ... because (say it out loud with me) it ALWAYS does!

Beau got engaged to the love of his life (not me) while I was busy writing the chapter on love. I found myself genuinely thrilled for him and for the love he was able to create with someone who is much better suited to him than I ever was. It felt like the completion of a chapter and a severing of energetic ties that had finally released me (and him) from those twin-flame shackles. Never in a million years did I think I'd react happily to the person I'd envisaged spending *my* life with ending up with someone else … like EVER! But when you raise your love vibrations, as I preach in the manifesting love chapter, and you find a completeness within yourself, then your past love stories are just that—stories, and you can easily separate the 'then' from the 'now'. If you relate to my history with Beau, and I know a tonne of you do, then please believe me when I say you will get out alive. You will find the love that you deserve, because you are already love.

I met with Beau days before I handed in the first draft of this book to my publisher. Not to ask for permission to include our story in the book, but to give him a heads up that he featured in it (because #therightthingtodo). Honestly, I predicted a reaction that I just didn't get. Past experience told me he would be offended, upset and disapproving, but he was none of those things. He was proud, excited and gave me his approval of both the content and his alias. This highlighted another lesson from the book: treat every experience as a new one, because when we go in with old stories, we're unable to grow and expand, and we keep experiences and people from our past stuck in the past, not allowing them to grow or expand, either.

While writing the opportunity chapter, I made a decision that went against my better judgment. Everything in my gut, my bones, my head and my heart told me it wasn't right, but convenience, finances and the happiness of my cat, Luna, meant that I ignored all of my instincts. The apartment that I'd inhabited for thirteen years was wearing thin, and I was over it. Energetically, I knew it was time to move on. Even so, I decided to keep the lease in my name for a few extra months so my beautiful friend and housemate, Jordan (this is actually her real name—it was confusing and equally hilarious!), wouldn't have to move out of our apartment near the beach just as summer was about to hit. Staying put also meant not having to find a solution for my Luna, who had unknowingly become collateral to my swift energetic ejection from said home. (Rehousing cats is a NIGHTMARE.)

I advertised for someone to fill my room and share the apartment with Jordan, and eventually we found a woman who was keen to move in. Although everything seemed to be falling into place, there was still a part of me that felt like this wasn't the solution. I knew I needed to cut all ties in order to be rid of the stuck energy that was still festering in that apartment, but I ignored the loud voices, heart pangs and gut gurgles because this felt like a convenient bandaid.

The day the new tenant was due to move in, she changed her mind. I had her bond (thank goodness) but it put Luna, Jordan and I right back at square one. I knew this was a push from the universe to terminate the lease and be done with it. Just like the shoulder dislocations, broken foot, cancelled flights and relationship breakdowns that I've discussed throughout this book, this was a symptom of me moving out of alignment with my intuition, ignoring my inner knowing and temporarily losing faith that the decision that satisfied my own authenticity would also be the right one for all parties involved, including Luna and Jords (the other one). #soconfusing

So yes, I got sideswiped when I ignored that really loud intuitive pang, but that was the lesson right there, and I tell you what—it didn't take me long to learn it and rectify the situation. As sure as you know when something is right, you know when something is not, and it's these instincts, nudges and symptoms from your inner knowing that transform a manifestation practice from sometimes getting it right to feeling confident that you—the complete and whole being that you are, right in this very moment—can Make It Happen, even if the 'right' choice is the toughest route.

As humans, we are innately creators. We create life, art, music, food, dance and connection, but every thought, feeling, vibration, colour and timeframe we experience is created by human interpretation. If you were to try to explain electricity, wi-fi or the Kardashians to our early ancestors, they wouldn't be able to fathom such advancements based on the evidence of the physical world they inhabited (sticks, stones and bony bums). But this is what manifestation is: having faith that anything is possible even when you can't see all of the evidence in front of you.

If we live life purely based on our past experiences and what we can see through our own tunnel vision, we risk living a very linear life. Humankind would not have progressed and expanded as it has if people hadn't been able to step outside of this.

Having devoured the pages of this book, you now know that your potential is far greater than anything your logical and rational mind interprets as data for creation. A simple shift in your thoughts and feelings can alter your vibrational frequency and have a profound ripple effect on how the rest of the world responds to you. Your actions can trigger profound changes that can shift your life trajectory in one fell swoop. Having faith in yourself and in the support of the universe might just be your greatest superpower.

The Manifestation Equation isn't something you just read about, learn the theory of and then forget about. Once you know it, you can't unknow it! If you've read every page and thought, 'I'll do the exercises later' or 'That one's irrelevant to me', I urge you to go back through and revisit them all. Each chapter in this book was written to deepen your relationship with numero uno—you. And just as each part of the equation is integral to manifestation, a strong sense of self-worth and belief in your own potential is integral for manifestation to work.

So together, let's revisit it all one more time, shall we?

Thoughts + Feelings + Actions + Faith = Successful manifestation

Remember, anything you want to manifest is possible when you apply the Manifestation Equation to it.

Thoughts: Are your thoughts aligned with what you want to manifest? If not, start by identifying the thoughts that are true. Anything else is irrelevant, and you can just let it go. The more you indulge the untrue thoughts, the more energy is wasted and the further away you get from realising your manifestations. Once you've sorted through your thoughts, you can move on to setting intentions.

Feelings: How will manifesting what you want make you feel? If you had what you wanted right now in the present moment, how would you feel? Place those feelings behind your intentions, and familiarise yourself with them. Feel into these feelings regularly. This is what will shift your vibration and attract the things you want towards you. Everything is energy and everything is vibrating on its own frequency, so nothing is out of your reach as long as you're vibrating on a similar frequency to whatever it is you want to attract, whether that's money, love, a career, opportunity, holidays ... anything!

Actions: You are the co-creator of your own future, so what can you start doing TODAY to get one step closer to your dreams? This includes taking responsibility for your past actions and having an awareness that YOU create your reality, so if something isn't working, do something about it! Please don't abandon the action step; it's the most important step of all. It is the clearest form of communication you can have with the universe, and if you do your bit, the universe will always meet you halfway. Remember, if you ever feel stuck, all you need to do to shift energy is MOVE.

Faith: The biggest hurdle I faced when writing this book was having faith —faith in myself, faith in the Manifestation Equation, faith in universal support and faith in the whole goddamn process. And when everything went to shit (which it did), I held on to that faith for dear life and it not only saved me from the depths of darkness, but it also allowed me to keep manifesting even when things appeared hopeless and impossibly flawed. Don't forget that faith dulls fear; when I feared being penniless, heartbroken and unattractive, faith in myself and the universe kept me neutral and unattached to the outcome, knowing that whatever manifested would be in my highest interest because I deserve nothing less, and neither do you. If you lose touch with your faith, go back to basics and look at every single universal cycle in existence as a reminder that there are ebbs and flows to everything. As sure as the sun rises, as sure as the seasons change and as sure as you will take your next inhale breath, there is always going to be more money, more love, more opportunity and more protein powder.

Want to hear a secret? This is actually a self-empowerment text disguised as a book about manifestation (insert evil laughter here). Because the natural and effortless by-product of loving, accepting and trusting yourself is that you can actually manifest anything you bloody well want. #lifehack

All of the answers, high vibrations and potential outcomes you're searching for are already brewing inside of you. The stronger your relationship is with yourself, the easier these things are to access. And that's all manifestation is: listening, feeling, acting and trusting from a place of inner knowing.

YOUR thoughts, YOUR feelings, YOUR actions and YOUR faith determine YOUR reality. The only thing you need to prioritise when learning how to manifest is you. When you can stand confidently in your own worthiness, tap into the essence of love that innately resides in you and have faith that you're always being fully supported, there is nothing that you can't create.

So go. Manifest. Make it happen.

Notes

Page 48 While it's hard to gather definitive and conclusive evidence when it comes to our thoughts …; Maria Millet, 31 March 2017, 'Challenge your negative thoughts', Michigan State University Extension, viewed 17 December 2018. <https://www.canr.msu.edu/news/challenge_your_negative_thoughts>.

Page 51 'As you think different thoughts, your brain circuits fire in corresponding sequences, patterns and combinations …'; Dr Joe Dispenza, *Breaking the Habit of Being Yourself: How to Lose Your Mind and Create a New One*, Hay House, California, 2012, p. 57.

Page 84 'While action is an important component in the physical world in which you are focused …'; Esther and Jerry Hicks, *The Law of Attraction: The basics of the Teachings of Abraham* (Kindle edition, location 1398), Hay House, California, 2006.

Page 112 'The ancients called the dark days …'; Bri. Maya Tiwari, *The Path of Practice: A Woman's Book of Ayurvedic Healing,* Ballantine Books, New York, 2000, p. 97.

Page 115 … 'the intake of cosmic energy by the individual for his growth and progress …'; B.K.S. Iyengar, *Light on Pranayama: The Definitive Guide to the Art of Breathing*, Allen & Unwin, London, 1981, pp. 114–115, 121.

Page 123 'the more often we define reality through our sense …'; Dr Joe Dispenza, op. cit., p. 106.

Page 123 'Basically, your fear is like a mall cop who thinks he's a Navy SEAL ...'; Elizabeth Gilbert, *Big Magic: Creative Living Beyond Fear*, Bloomsbury Publishing, London, 2015, p. 23.

Page 135 'We should never be able to predict how our new creations will manifest; they must catch us off guard.' Dr Joe Dispenza op. cit., p. 24.

Page 139 'Can you give thanks for something ...'; Dr Joe Dispenza op.cit., p. 26.

Page 223 'We are shaped by the love narratives that we read ...'; Alain de Botton, 'On Love', Talk and Ideas Event at Sydney Opera House, July 2016, <http://www.yousubtitles.com/Alain-de-Botton-On-Love-Sydney-Opera-House-id-1214991>.

Page 233 'A soul contract usually has a few different premises ...'; Matt Kahn via YouTube; July 8 2015; <https://www.youtube.com/watch?v=n2da2CQEyy0>.

Page 236 'The twin flame brings up in you the betrayal, the disillusionment, the confusion, the heartbreak ...'; Matt Kahn via YouTube; July 8 2015; <https://www.youtube.com/watch?v=n2da2CQEyy0>.

Links to guided meditations:

http://jordannalevin.com/make-it-happen-bonuses/

Thank you

I can't be sure, but I reckon most authors mentally write their thank you pages long before their first book idea is even conceived. I imagine the same can be said for an actor's Oscar speech, a musician's Grammy award acceptance and the scientist or humanitarian who dreams of winning the Nobel Peace Prize. (Note: I'm not comparing myself to Meryl Streep, John Legend or Al Gore … much.)

In some form or another, I wrote this thank you page before the majority of the people in it were even part of my life, let alone part of the book-writing process, so in a way this thank you page not only manifested the book it will now be included in, but all of the people who have become such an integral part of it.

The exceptions to this are, of course, my parents, who I guess, in a way, manifested me.

My mother, Trishaa; the hippie, mentor, writer, editor, reviewer and mediator. My biggest cheerleader, someone who always endeavours to give an unbiased review of my work but can't help muddling that up with pride, unconditional love and the vision of me as a three-year-old sharing her first finger painting. I undoubtedly could never have believed in myself as much as I do without your unwavering belief in my infinite potential, always.

My father, Rhon; the practical, supportive, rational and logical coach who always helps me keep my eye on the prize. Your offer to help me type up the first draft will go down in history as the least helpful way you could lend your support, since your typing speed is close to 10 words a minute (with one finger), but it was the most beautiful gesture and maybe one day I'll take you up on it. Thank you for putting a roof over my head when I decided that I needed to get out of my apartment 'to move around stuck energy' and allowing me to store six tubs in the garage when I told you there'd only be two.

Then, of course, there is the support team behind both of them. We didn't quite explore the quirkiness and expansiveness of my modern family in this book, but my step-parents, the other halves to my birth parents, both deserve a special mention for making my parents happy and showing me what love looks like, even though I could (but choose not to) play out the story of a child from a broken home.

So to Mum's husband, Garry, I say thank you for keeping her grounded, safe and blissfully happy, and to my stepmother, Donna, thank you for loving me like your own blood from the age of four and backing me and my preposterously large dreams. (We will build that yurt.)

I believe I manifested every single one of my amazing and supportive friends, and without them this book would not have been possible. Extra-special mentions go to:

Cassie, words will never be able to express how grateful I am for your friendship. Your support, advice, laughter and lunch dates made the book-writing process seamless. Thank you for your effervescent use of emojis, your unwavering lifting up of my ego, and always laughing at my jokes (also great for said ego).

Jo, our daily walks kept me sane, especially when deep in the final chapters of this book. I still believe that our expertly crafted walking route through the affluent eastern suburbs of Sydney has created a vibrational frequency that will have us both living the mansion life in the not-too-distant future. Your advice regarding writing a book and the publishing industry was priceless, and I'm so grateful that adversity in the workplace brought us together. Also, I really appreciate you letting me practise my stand-up routines on you. Between you and Cassie, I've pretty much convinced myself I'm the next Jerry Seinfeld.

Laura, you are my everything. My rock, my business coach, my best friend and my sister. Thank you for believing in me, encouraging me and giving me the space to vent, cry and throw in the towel, and then eloquently talk me back off the ledge.

Zoe, you are my soul sister and confidante, but also my energetic healer and kinesiologist. When I say the words in this book wouldn't be possible without you, I believe that with every cell in my body. Thank you for clearing old stories that kept me stuck, aligning me with my purpose and teaching me your witchy ways so that I was able to say what needed to be said, and do what needed to be done. I thank the universe every day for bringing you into my orbit.

Big shout out to Jordan, who had the 'pleasure' of sharing a home with me during the book-writing process. Thank you for letting me turn our hallway into *A Beautiful Mind* meets *Good Will Hunting* mind map, for listening to me freak out about deadlines every other day and for being a shining light in my home for the last few months of what was an epic 13-year stint.

Beau (not your real name, but you know who you are), thank you for letting me share our story so that it can help others grow and find the love they deserve. You've always been in my corner, and your grace, kindness and support towards me and this book is appreciated more than you will ever know. Also thanks for sharing your prize money with me that one time we were on *Deal or No Deal*; it's hands-down one of my favourite party stories.

My support team also extends to Amy, Ruby, Brittany, Megsie, the Spirit Sisters, Vicki, Emma, Cherida, Aiyana and Zac. Whether it was phone chats, glasses of wine or words of encouragement, you all kept me on purpose, and I hope everyone manifests connections like yours.

This book would never have existed without the success of my event series Lunar Nights, and Lunar Nights would never have been a success without the beautiful attendees who show up every month to set their intentions under a new moon and manifest their deepest desires and wildest dreams. Thank you for showing up each month and exploring your own vulnerability among a conscious collective.

Thank you to my wonderful peers and colleagues, Charlie de Haas, Cassie Mendoza-Jones, Amy Molloy, Melissa Ambrosini, Katie Manitsas and Hollie Azzopardi, who took the time to read the first draft of this book, while it was still littered with spelling mistakes and grammatical errors. Your kind words, camaraderie, and ability to support another woman in a similar industry brings me to happy tears.

A huge thank you to Murdoch Books, and especially to my publisher, Kelly Doust. Thank you for taking a chance on this first-time author and believing in my book from the very first pitch until the very last edit. Thank you for your patience while I changed my mind a zillion times, and for your honesty when I handed in a final chapter that was way below my potential. Kelly, your warmth, support, advice and encouragement will forever shape the experience that has been writing my first book, and I believe it's no accident that we ended up together birthing this book into the world. To the editors, designers and sales and marketing teams at Murdoch, who make the book-creating process appear seamless even though it's far from it, thank you for holding my hand and imparting your time and wisdom on this project.

Last but not least, thanks to all of you—the readers, the keen manifestors and the dreamers. You are about to embark on a life-changing journey, and all I ask is that you believe that you are capable of manifesting everything you desire.

Index